T0334160

# The Problem of China

**'China, by her resources and her population, is capable of being the greatest power in the world after the United States.'**
Bertrand Russell, *The Problem of China*

In 1920 the philosopher Bertrand Russell spent a year in China as Professor of Philosophy at the University of Beijing (then Peking), where his lectures on mathematical logic enthralled students and listeners, including Mao Tse Tung, who attended some of Russell's talks. Written at a time when China was largely regarded by the West as backward and weak, *The Problem of China* sees Russell rise above the prejudices of his era and presciently assess China's past, present and future.

Russell brings his analytical and insightful eye to bear on some fundamental aspects of China's history and politics, cautioning China against adopting a purely Western model of social and economic development, which he regarded as characterized by a combination of greed and militarism. Beginning with an overview of nineteenth-century Chinese history and considering China's relations with Japan and Russia, Russell then contrasts Chinese civilization with Western. He devotes a fascinating chapter to the character of the Chinese, which he argues is complex but ultimately defined by a 'pacific temper'.

With uncanny foresight, Russell predicts China's resurgence, but only if it is able to establish an orderly government, promote industrial development under Chinese control and foster the spread of education.

This Routledge Classics edition includes a new introduction by Bernard Linsky.

**Bertrand Russell** (1872–1970) is regarded as one of the greatest philosophers of the twentieth century, a celebrated writer and commentator on social and political affairs.

Routledge Classics contains the very best of Routledge publishing over the past century or so, books that have, by popular consent, become established as classics in their field. Drawing on a fantastic heritage of innovative writing published by Routledge and its associated imprints, this series makes available in attractive, affordable form some of the most important works of modern times.

For a complete list of titles visit:
https://www.routledge.com/Routledge-Classics/book-series/SE0585

Bertrand
# Russell

## The Problem of China

With a new introduction by Bernard Linsky

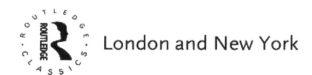 London and New York

First published in Routledge Classics 2021
by Routledge
2 Park Square, Milton Park, Abingdon, Oxon OX14 4RN

and by Routledge
52 Vanderbilt Avenue, New York, NY 10017

*Routledge is an imprint of the Taylor & Francis Group, an informa business*

© 2021 Bertrand Russell Peace Foundation Ltd

Introduction to the Routledge Classics edition © 2021 Bernard Linsky

The right of the Bertrand Russell Peace Foundation Ltd to be identified as author of this work has been asserted by them in accordance with sections 77 and 78 of the Copyright, Designs and Patents Act 1988.

First published by George Allen & Unwin Ltd 1922

*British Library Cataloguing-in-Publication Data*
A catalogue record for this book is available from the British Library

*Library of Congress Cataloging-in-Publication Data*
A catalog record has been requested for this book

ISBN: 978-0-367-54732-5 (hbk)
ISBN: 978-0-367-54080-7 (pbk)
ISBN: 978-1-003-09034-2 (ebk)

Typeset in Joanna
by codeMantra

# CONTENTS

# Introduction to the Routledge Classics Edition

Bertrand Russell completed *The Problem of China* in the first months of 1922 to report on the current state of China in international relations. He had just returned from ten months in Beijing, originally to lecture on philosophy at Peking University but then increasingly to address eager audiences about how to modernize their new republic. Russell returned full of admiration for the culture and values of traditional China and with the advice about their future that he reports here. In addition to giving three academic lecture courses and meeting with academic study groups, he was invited to address a variety of audiences in the city and met with prominent intellectuals and politicians. Russell, not yet divorced from his first wife Alys, was accompanied by his new lover Dora Black, who lectured to various groups on education and social issues. They lived openly unmarried – alarming the British diplomatic corps – with their interpreter and some domestic servants in a traditional courtyard house in an alley hutong east of the Forbidden City. Russell settled in Beijing early in November of 1920, and then spent the next months giving more than 60 lectures. Russell's lecturing ended abruptly in February 1921 when he was hospitalized with pneumonia so severe that reports of his death circulated in European newspapers. A long convalescence ended any public talks until a parting address in July, after which the couple left for Japan on their way home to Britain via the Pacific Ocean and a train across Canada.

For the Beijing lectures, a junior professor, the Harvard-educated philosopher and linguist Zhao Yuanren, interpreted as Russell spoke and accompanied him to meetings with leading intellectuals. The visit was a cause of great excitement. Over 1,000 people were in the overflowing audience for the first of 14 weekly lectures on "The Problems of Philosophy". Peking University published a *Russell Monthly* and created a discussion society. Russell also gave a synopsis of *The Analysis of Mind* in another lecture series, and had just started a series of four introductory lectures on mathematical logic when he was cut short by his illness. In between there were many lectures and addresses to various audiences around the city on topics such as ethics, Einstein's theory of relativity, conditions in Russia and religious belief, and a lecture to the embassy of the Far Eastern Soviet Republic. The university lectures updated Russell's new "scientific philosophy" to adapt to developments in physics from relativity theory and quantum theory. These are only now being translated into English and will be of interest to English speakers who follow Russell's technical philosophy. English speakers have all along had access to the lectures on social and political topics, as there were four chapters on socialism and imperialism in the book that Russell published with Dora in 1923, *Prospects for Industrial Civilization*, and in sections of *The Problem of China*. What we can learn about the revival of Russell's reputation in China is perhaps a more important reason to study these books anew.

In the second half of the fifty years since Russell's death, his reputation in the anglophone world may also be recovering from a low period following Ray Monk's influential but devastating biography. Academic philosophers had treated Russell's turn to public philosophy as a new career, leaving behind his analytic philosophy to others. Monk criticized Russell's public writings as a feeble "journalism" marred by his lack of empathy for his own loved ones and lack of moral conviction. Perhaps now, fifty years after his death, and in the face of a rehabilitation of his reputation in China, a fresh look at the reprinting of the "popular philosophy" books will allow anglophone philosophers and intellectuals outside of academia to reassess Russell's legacy.

Bertrand Russell completed *The Problem of China* in May of 1922 as the victors of the First World War turned their attention to the balance of power in the Pacific. The United States, Britain, Japan, France and Italy met in Washington to split up the spoils of the war, awarding Russian and German territory to Japan and confirming British rule in Hong Kong until 1997. The Versailles conference three years before had given the German treaty port Tsingdao to Japan. The Russians and Japanese divided Manchuria. In response, foreign-educated Chinese students led violent protests, launching the May Fourth Movement based in the universities. By 1926, Russell was able to report in a postscript that Tsingdao would after all be returned to China, but that there was little else that suggested a change in the aggressive attitude of Japan. Russell's fears were confirmed by the Japanese invasion of Manchuria in 1931 and the long descent into the Second World War.

This amusing and stylishly written book was prescient in foreseeing the threat of another war if conflicts with Japan could not be overcome in the 1920s. Yet it is just as relevant today as there is still a problem of how to respond to China in world politics and economics. One hundred years ago China and Japan were already hostile rivals, although Korea was under Japanese domination and China was an impoverished subject of Western imperial powers. Russell charges that the West wanted to prevent the development of local industry to rival imports. Railways and mines, which he deemed essential for the first steps of industrialization, were directly operated by the Japanese or indebted to Western investors. China is now the largest manufacturing economy in the world, yet we find it seeking to keep control over foreign joint ventures, and resenting tariffs designed to curtail its industry. As a result of the Washington Conference the Japanese left Tsingdao and split Manchuria with the Soviet Union, but kept all of Korea and Taiwan — areas that China still takes to be in its sphere of influence. The British kept Hong Kong, but only until 1997, and today we see the street protests over the One China policy of unification. The Americans, who did not demand control of territory, instead favoured their Open China policy, combining free trade for their imports with tariffs on Chinese manufacturing. In 1922, China was still in the midst of anarchy and civil war among different regions, lacking a strong and unified government. All of these issues in China's foreign policy predate the very founding of the Communist Party of China and long civil war that concluded with Mao Zedong's proclamation o f the People's Republic of China in 1949. The problem the West had with China in 1922 seems to be still unfolding today.

Russell had travelled in the preceding year through Soviet Russia but it was China that touched him personally:

> one of the most memorable things about the Chinese is their power of securing the affection of foreigners. Almost all Europeans like China, both those who have come only as tourists and those who live here for many years. ... Those who have lived long among them tend to acquire their outlook and their standards. New arrivals are struck by the obvious evils: the beggars, the terrible poverty, the prevalence of disease, the anarchy and corruption in politics. Every energetic Westerner feels at first a strong desire to reform these evils, and of course they ought to be reformed.

Russell had not reacted that way to the people of Russia, even independently of his horror at the Bolshevik dictatorship. He was not oblivious to the dire situation of China, yet he was in love with China. The visit was obviously a release for Russell after the horrors of the recent war. Yet the same awareness of his status as an outsider with much to learn from a new culture is followed immediately by a characteristic irony that is interpreted by many as a cringe-worthy lack of moral sensibility:

> But the Chinese, even those who are the victims of preventable misfortunes, show a vast passive indifference to the excitement of foreigners;

they wait for it to go off, like the effervescence of soda-water. And gradually strange hesitations creep into the mind of the bewildered traveller; after a period of indignation, he begins to doubt all the maxims he
has hitherto accepted without question. Is it really wise to be always
guarding against future misfortune? Is it prudent to lose all enjoyment
that may come at some future date? Should our lives be passed in
building a mansion that we shall never have leisure to inhabit?

The Chinese answer these questions in the negative, and therefore
have to put up with poverty, disease, and anarchy. But, to compensate
for these evils, they have retained, as industrial nations have not, the
capacity for civilized enjoyment, for leisure and laughter, for pleasure
in sunshine and philosophical discourse.

The sympathetic reader should bear each of these passages by focussing
on the immediately following contrasts with the West, where passivity
is contrasted with restless energy aimed at domination, and backward-
ness with the terrible "efficiency at homicide" of self-assertive, industrialized, nations. An understanding of Russell's recent experiences in
the war makes sense of his odd sounding list of "the chief defects of
the Chinese" in a familiar triad: "avarice, cowardice, and callousness".
In Russell's hands these three faults of Victorian morals become sum-
maries of virtues. The "avarice" refers to the private life of commerce
that places the support of the material needs of family ahead of fanatical commitment to national ideology. The poor military success
of mercenary Chinese armies that would run from battles with few
casualties echoes Russell's own pacifism in the preceding war where
conscientious objectors were condemned as "cowards". The "callousness" in the face of disease and famine is not unique to the Chinese,
but shared by foreigners as well, only to be rejected in the elevation of
the welfare of peasants in the ideology of the Communist party.

The characteristically witty and sometimes sarcastic survey of the
history of China finds three distinctive cultural features that explain its
long survival as a unified empire:

The use of ideograms (characters) instead of an alphabet in writing;
(2) the substitution of the Confucian ethic for religion among the

educated classes; (3) government by literati chosen by examination instead of by a hereditary aristocracy.

Given his philosophical work as a founder of mathematical symbolic logic, Russell was naturally fascinated with the written Chinese language. Instead of using an alphabet, the language was written with strings of abstract pictorial characters, each one representing the same meaning across mutually unintelligible spoken languages. He saw this common written language as an important source of the unity of Chinese culture and two-thousand-year history of a unified state when the West saw the rise and fall of different nations. Russell repeatedly describes the Chinese as "aesthetic", having retained a sense of beauty that was immune to the frantic busyness of the West. This is attributed to the Daoist tradition of seeking "production without possession, action without self-assertion, development without domination". He is not blind to failings of the ancient Chinese way of life and repeatedly stresses the need for China to make up for its failure to develop empirical science. The widespread corruption of Chinese officials is explained as descended from the laudable Confucian ethics of loyalty to family that made it the duty of public figures to provide for their extended family or clan, and so less pernicious than its Western version. Russell slyly defends a bureaucracy of literary scholars who passed civil service examinations on the literary classics by comparing it with the British history of rule by a monarch and aristocracy:

> Aristocracy, in our sense of the word, came to an end before the beginning of the Christian era, and government was in the hands of officials chosen for proficiency in writing in a dead language, as in England.

These first chapters are the basis of the consequent plea to those Western powers who were deciding what to do with Japanese demands, urging them to let China educate its people in Western science and industrialize, taking the best from the West but maintaining its traditional values and culture as far as possible.

The visit to China that produced this book marked a change in Russell's life and career, from Cambridge don to the public intellectual and peace activist he was to be until his death in 1970. In the first decades of the twentieth century Russell had created the new academic school of Analytic Philosophy with G.E. Moore and Ludwig Wittgenstein at Cambridge University. Horrified by the outpouring of public enthusiasm at the outbreak of the First World War, Russell became deeply involved in the resistance to conscription. A public campaign of speeches, letters and leafletting against conscription led to a conviction under the Defense of the Realm Act, his scandalous dismissal from Cambridge University in 1916 and finally imprisonment for five months in 1918 at the end of the war. Now out of work, and outraged by the consequences of the war, Russell visited Soviet Russia during the summer of 1920, travelling alongside a Labour Party delegation. On his return from Russia Russell found an invitation to lecture by the Chinese Lecture Association, an affiliate of the May Fourth Movement at Peking University. He immediately accepted and set out on the six-week sea voyage with Dora Black, who had just been in Russia as well. Waiting for their ship in Marseilles, Russell completed the manuscript of *The Practice and Theory of Bolshevism*. It was a disappointment that this book offended everyone he knew: conservatives, with its sympathy for the Russian Revolution, the separate peace, and communism in the form of "state socialism", and the Left by his criticisms of Bolshevism as a dictatorship using cruel and oppressive methods. Russell was convinced of the importance of a humane ideal in history and politics and not just the economic material forces or political realist dogmas of others on both the Right and Left. Russell's particular combination of enthusiasm for socialism in the economy where all manufacturing and other industry including railways are to be owned by the state, with an abhorrence of the dictatorship of Lenin's Bolshevik "dictatorship of the proletariat", gained few adherents in China. Throughout Russell praises the dedication of the Chinese to their private interests, unfettered by the demands of government or religion.

After his return to Britain in the fall of 1921, Russell finalized his divorce from Alys, and married Dora just before the birth of his first child, John. The success of several periodical articles in Britain and the U.S. published immediately after his return then inspired him to reformulate his ideas for *The Problem of China*.

The American pragmatist philosopher and educational reformer John Dewey was in China from April of 1919 to July of 1921. Dewey urged the importance of education for the modernization of China, which Russell praised. Russell, however, seems to have soured on Dewey, and makes several remarks about him as advancing the American approach to China. Americans, Russell found, were happy with an independent China as long as it remained open to their trade and investment. He satirizes these missionaries for Americanism promoting "clean living, clean thinking, and pep" which in effect amount to

> the substitution of tidiness for art, cleanliness for beauty, moralizing for philosophy, prostitutes for concubines (as being easier to conceal), and a general air of being frightfully busy for the leisurely calm of the traditional Chinese.

Despite Russell's scorn Dewey seems to have had more of a lasting influence on China with his progressive elementary education that survived into the era of the People's Republic.

In a stop-over in the city of Changsa days after arriving in China, on his way to Beijing from Shanghai, Russell presented his views on Russia over four lectures in 24 hours, speaking on "Bolshevism and World Politics". The Chinese report of the lectures, as yet unavailable in English, was signed under a pseudonym of Mao Zedong, a year before the founding of the Chinese Communist Party, when there was not yet a settled view on what was to be learned from Russia. Mao described the lectures in a letter in December of 1920 reporting on his debates with four comrades:

> In his lectures at Changsa, Russell, who shared the same view with Zisheng and Hesheng, took a position in favor of communism but against the dictatorship of the proletariat. He argued that that it is

acceptable to employ the method of education to inspire the bour- geoise without interfering with freedom, triggering wars, or causing bloody revolutions. But after Russell's lectures I had an extensive dis- pute with Yinbai and Lirong, among others, and my comments on Russell's views can be summarized in two sentences: [Russell's view] is sound in theory. But it doesn't work in practice.

Mao argues that no amount of education or parliamentary reform will persuade the capitalist bourgeoise to surrender their control of the army and police to the oppressed proletariat. The Soviet model was from then onwards the only route to Communism.

In the twenty-first century Russell's reputation in China is being rehabilitated. Although Russell had mediated an exchange of views between Nehru and Zhou Enlai during the Indo-Chinese border dis- pute of the early 1960s, and his philosophical works, especially his world-wide best seller *The History of Western Philosophy*, have long been available in translation, the social and political views of the lectures were classed with "bourgeois liberals" through the Maoist era. Mao had long been aware of the views in *The Problem of China* on individual liberty and freedom ever since the lectures at Changsa. The Commu- nist Party of China was openly modelled on the Bolshevik Revolution in Russia from its founding in 1921. Even so, some ethical essays have been included in set texts for school students across the country. A na- tional publishing house is preparing a critical edition of the periodical reports of Russell's lectures and addresses, including the Changsa lec- tures on Bolshevism, along with the first back-translation into English. Russell's proposal that China develop a socialist industrial economy of scientifically educated people motivated by a non-religious Confucian social ethic now seems to be national economic policy. At the opening session of the 2018 World Congress of Philosophy in the Great Hall of the People in Beijing, under the Confucian slogan of "Learning to be Human", it was obvious that the national leadership is looking for a new post-Maoist national philosophy stressing commitment to the common good to temper the individualism at the base of the new competitive economy, all still under the control of a strong central government. Despite his repudiation of the Bolshevist dictatorship and his praise for the individual liberty of traditional culture, something in Russell's views has struck a chord in China. After some years languishing out of fashion, both in China and in the West, it is refreshing to reread *The Problem of China* as the Western world once again faces these familiar problems and to speculate on what the Chinese find appealing in Russell's philosophy.

Bernard Linsky

# Preface

This book is reprinted unchanged, although it was written in 1922 and hardly anything has remained unchanged during the intervening forty-three years. Much of the book is topical and could only be adapted to the present day by alterations which would have completely transformed it. It seemed better, therefore, to make no attempt at modernizing the book, but to preserve that measure of historical truth which belongs to a record of dead hopes and dead fears. The parts which are not topical still seem to me, in the main, correct. I would mention, in particular, the contrast of the traditional Chinese character and the character of powerful Western nations. There is, however, one large difference between the China of that day and the China of the present. The China of that day was threatened mainly by the ambitions of Japan, but these ambitions perished in the Hiroshima bomb. Other bombs now threaten China, and other means of protection must be sought by the Chinese. Purged by misfortune and saved by their own heroism, they deserve success. May it be theirs!

Bertrand Russell
Plas Penrhyn, 9 November, 1965

# 1

---

# QUESTIONS

A European lately arrived in China, if he is of a receptive and reflective disposition, finds himself confronted with a number of very puzzling questions, for many of which the problems of Western Europe will not have prepared him. Russian problems, it is true, have important affinities with those of China, but they have also important differences; moreover they are decidedly less complex. Chinese problems, even if they affected no one outside China, would be of vast importance, since the Chinese are estimated to constitute about a quarter of the human race. In fact, however, all the world will be vitally affected by the development of Chinese affairs, which may well prove a decisive factor, for good or evil, during the next two centuries. This makes it important, to Europe and America almost as much as to Asia, that there should be an intelligent understanding of the questions raised by China, even if, as yet, definite answers are difficult to give.

The questions raised by the present condition of China fall naturally into three groups, economic, political, and cultural. No one of these groups, however, can be considered in isolation, because each is intimately bound up with the other two. For my part, I think the cultural questions are the most important, both for China and for mankind; if these could be solved, I would accept, with more or less equanimity, any political or economic system which ministered to that end. Unfortunately, however, cultural questions have little interest for practical men, who regard money and power as the proper ends for nations as for individuals. The helplessness of the artist in a hard-headed business community has long been a commonplace of novelists and moralizers, and has made collectors feel virtuous when they bought up the pictures of painters who had died in penury. China may be regarded as an artist nation, with the virtues and vices to be expected of the artist: virtues chiefly useful to others, and vices chiefly harmful to oneself. Can Chinese virtues be preserved? Or must China, in order to survive, acquire, instead, the vices which make for success and cause misery to others only? And if China does copy the model set by all foreign nations with which she has dealings, what will become of all of us?

China has an ancient civilization which is now undergoing a very rapid process of change. The traditional civilization of China had developed in almost complete independence of Europe, and had merits and demerits quite different from those of the West. It would be futile to attempt to strike a balance; whether our present culture is better or worse, on the whole, than that which seventeenth-century missionaries found in the Celestial Empire is a question as to which no prudent person would venture to pronounce. But it is easy to point to certain respects in which we are better than old China, and to other respects in which we are worse. If intercourse between Western nations and China is to be fruitful, we must cease to regard ourselves as missionaries of a superior civilization, or, worse still, as men who have a right to exploit, oppress, and swindle the Chinese because they are an "inferior" race. I do not see any reason to believe that the Chinese are inferior to ourselves; and I think most Europeans, who have any intimate knowledge of China, would take the same view.

In comparing an alien culture with one's own, one is forced to ask oneself questions more fundamental than any that usually arise in regard to home affairs. One is forced to ask: What are the things that I ultimately value? What would make me judge one sort of society more desirable than another sort? What sort of ends should I most wish to see realized in the world? Different people will answer these questions differently, and I do not know of any argument by which I could persuade a man who gave an answer different from my own. I must therefore be content merely to state the answer which appeals to me, in the hope that the reader may feel likewise.

The main things which seem to me important on their own account, and not merely as means to other things, are: knowledge, art, instinctive happiness, and relations of friendship or affection. When I speak of knowledge, I do not mean all knowledge; there is much in the way of dry lists of facts that is merely useful, and still more that has no appreciable value of any kind. But the understanding of Nature, incomplete as it is, which is to be derived from science, I hold to be a thing which is good and delightful on its own account. The same may be said, I think, of some biographies and parts of history. To enlarge on this topic would, however, take me too far from my theme. When I speak of art as one of the things that have value on their own account, I do not mean only the deliberate productions of trained artists, though of course these, at their best, deserve the highest place. I mean also the almost unconscious effort after beauty which one finds among Russian peasants and Chinese coolies, the sort of impulse that creates folk-songs, that existed among ourselves before the time of the Puritans, and survives in cottage gardens. Instinctive happiness, or joy of life, is one of the most important widespread popular goods that we have lost through industrialism and the high pressure at which most of us live; its commonness in China is a strong reason for thinking well of Chinese civilization.

In judging of a community, we have to consider, not only how much of good or evil there is within the community, but also what effects it has in promoting good or evil in other communities, and how far the good things which it enjoys depend upon evils elsewhere. In this respect, also, China is better than we are. Our prosperity, and most of what we endeavour to secure for ourselves, can only be obtained by widespread oppression and exploitation of weaker nations, while the Chinese are not strong enough to injure other countries, and secure whatever they enjoy by means of their own merits and exertions alone.

These general ethical considerations are by no means irrelevant in considering the practical problems of China. Our industrial and commercial civilization has been both the effect and the cause of certain more or less unconscious beliefs as to what is worth while; in China one becomes conscious of these beliefs through the spectacle of a society which challenges them by being built, just as unconsciously, upon a different standard of values. Progress and efficiency, for example, make no appeal to the Chinese, except to those who have come under Western influence. By valuing progress and efficiency, we have secured power and wealth; by ignoring them, the Chinese, until we brought disturbance, secured on the whole a peaceable existence and a life full of enjoyment. It is difficult to compare these opposite achievements unless we have some standard of values in our minds; and unless it is a more or less conscious standard, we shall undervalue the less familiar civilization, because evils to which we are not accustomed always make a stronger impression than those that we have learned to take as a matter of course.

The culture of China is changing rapidly, and undoubtedly rapid change is needed. The change that has hitherto taken place is traceable ultimately to the military superiority of the West; but in future our economic superiority is likely to be quite as potent. I believe that, if the Chinese are left free to assimilate what they want of our civilization, and to reject what strikes them as bad, they will be able to achieve an organic growth from their own tradition, and to produce a very splendid result, combining our merits with theirs. There are, however, two opposite dangers to be avoided if this is to happen. The first danger is that they may become completely Westernized, retaining nothing of what has hitherto distinguished them, adding merely one more to the restless, intelligent, industrial, and militaristic-nations which now afflict this unfortunate planet. The second danger is that they may be driven, in the course of resistance to foreign aggression, into an intense anti-foreign conservatism as regards everything except armaments. This has happened in Japan, and it may easily happen in China. The future of Chinese culture is intimately bound up with political and economic questions; and it is through their influence that dangers arise.

China is confronted with two very different groups of foreign Powers, on the one hand the white nations, on the other hand Japan. In considering the effect of the white races on the Far East as a whole, modern Japan must count as a Western product; therefore the responsibility for Japan's doings in China rests ultimately with her white teachers. Nevertheless, Japan remains very unlike Europe and America, and has ambitions different from theirs as regards China. We must therefore distinguish three possibilities: (1) China may become enslaved to one or more white nations; (2) China may become enslaved to Japan; (3) China may recover and retain her liberty. Temporarily there is a fourth possibility, namely that a consortium of Japan and the White Powers may control China; but I do not believe that, in the long run, the Japanese will be able to co-operate with England and America. In the long run, I believe that Japan must dominate the Far East or go under. If the Japanese had a different character this would not be the case; but the nature of their ambitions makes them exclusive and un-neighbourly. I shall give the reasons for this view when I come to deal with the relations of China and Japan.

To understand the problem of China, we must first know something of Chinese history and culture before the irruption of the white man, then something of modern Chinese culture and its inherent tendencies; next, it is necessary to deal in outline with the military and diplomatic relations of the Western Powers with China, beginning with our war of 1840 and ending with the treaty concluded after the Boxer rising of 1900. Although the Sino-Japanese war comes in this period, it is possible to separate, more or less, the actions of Japan in that war, and to see what system the White Powers would have established if Japan had not existed. Since that time, however, Japan has been the dominant foreign influence in Chinese affairs. It is therefore necessary to understand how the Japanese became what they are: what sort of nation they were before the West destroyed their isolation, and what influence the West has had upon them. Lack of understanding of Japan has made people in England blind to Japan's aims in China, and unable to apprehend the meaning of what Japan has done.

Political considerations alone, however, will not suffice to explain what is going on in relation to China; economic questions are almost more important. China is as yet hardly industrialized, and is certainly the most important undeveloped area left in the world. Whether the resources of China are to be developed by China, by Japan, or by the white races, is a question of enormous importance, affecting not only the whole development of Chinese civilization, but the balance of power in the world, the prospects of peace, the destiny of Russia, and the chances of development towards a better economic system in the advanced nations.

The Washington Conference has partly exhibited and partly concealed the conflict for the possession of China between nations all of which have guaranteed China's independence and integrity. Its outcome has made it far more difficult than before to give a hopeful answer as regards Far Eastern problems, and in particular as regards the question: Can China preserve any shadow of independence without a great development of nationalism and militarism? I cannot bring myself to advocate nationalism and militarism, yet it is difficult to know what to say to patriotic Chinese who ask how they can be avoided. So far, I have found only one answer. The Chinese nation is the most patient in the world; it thinks of centuries as other nations think of decades. It is essentially indestructible, and can afford to wait. The "civilized" nations of the world, with their blockades, their poison gases, their bombs, sub-marines, and negro armies, will probably destroy each other within the next hundred years, leaving the stage to those whose pacifism has kept them alive, though poor and powerless. If China can avoid being goaded into war, her oppressors may wear themselves out in the end, and leave the Chinese free to pursue humane ends, instead of the war and rapine and destruction which all white nations love. It is perhaps a slender hope for China, and for ourselves it is little better than despair. But unless the Great Powers learn some moderation and some tolerance, I do not see any better possibility, though I see many that are worse.

Our Western civilization is built upon assumptions which, to a psychologist, are rationalizings of excessive energy. Our industrialism, our militarism, our love of progress, our missionary zeal, our imperialism, our passion for dominating and organizing, all spring from a superflux of the itch for activity. The creed of efficiency for its own sake, without regard for the ends to which it is directed, has become somewhat discredited in Europe since the war, which would have never taken place if the Western nations had been slightly more indolent. But in America this creed is still almost universally accepted; so it is in Japan, and so it is by the Bolsheviks, who have been aiming fundamentally at the Americanization of Russia. Russia, like China, may be described as an artist nation; but unlike China it has been governed, since the time of Peter the Great, by men who wished to introduce all the good and evil of the West. In former days, I might have had no doubt that such men were in the right. Some (though not many) of the Chinese returned students resemble them in the belief that Western push and hustle are the most desirable things on earth. I cannot now take this view. The evils produced in China by indolence seem to me far less disastrous, from the point of view of mankind at large, than those produced throughout the world by the domineering cocksureness of Europe and America. The Great War showed that something is wrong with our civilization; experience of Russia and China has made me believe that those countries can help to show us what it is that is wrong. The Chinese have discovered, and have practised for many centuries, a way of life which, if it could be adopted by all the world, would make all the world happy. We Europeans have not. Our way of life demands strife, exploitation, restless change, discontent and destruction. Efficiency directed to destruction can only end in annihilation, and it is to this consummation that our civilization is tending, if it cannot learn some of that wisdom for which it despises the East.

It was on the Volga, in the summer of 1920, that I first realized how profound is the disease in our Western mentality, which the Bolsheviks are attempting to force upon an essentially Asiatic population, just as Japan and the West are doing in China. Our boat travelled on, day after day, through an unknown and mysterious land. Our company were noisy, gay, quarrelsome, full of facile theories, with glib explanations of everything, persuaded that there is nothing they could not understand and no human destiny outside the purview of their system. One of us lay at death's door, fighting a grim battle with weakness and terror and the indifference of the strong, assailed day and night by the sounds of loud-voiced love-making and trivial laughter. And all around us lay a great silence, strong as death, unfathomable as the heavens. It seemed that none had leisure to hear the silence, yet it called to me so insistently that I grew deaf to the harangues of propagandists and the endless information of the well-informed.

One night, very late, our boat stopped in a desolate spot where there were no houses, but only a great sandbank, and beyond it a row of poplars with the rising moon behind them. In silence I went ashore, and found on the sand a strange assemblage of human beings, half-nomads, wandering from some remote region of famine, each family huddled together surrounded by all its belongings, some sleeping, others silently making small fires of twigs. The flickering flames lighted up gnarled, bearded faces of wild men, strong, patient, primitive women, and children as sedate and slow as their parents. Human beings they undoubtedly were, and yet it would have been far easier for me to grow intimate with a dog or a cat or a horse than with one of them. I knew that they would wait there day after day, perhaps for weeks, until a boat came in which they could go to some distant place in which they had heard—falsely perhaps—that the earth was more generous than in the country they had left. Some would die by the way, all would suffer hunger and thirst and the scorching mid-day sun, but their sufferings would be dumb. To me they seemed to typify the very soul of Russia, unexpressive, inactive from despair, unheeded by the little set of Westernizers who make up all the parties of progress or reaction. Russia is so vast that the articulate few are lost in it as man and his planet are lost in interstellar space. It is possible, I thought, that the theorists may increase the misery of the many by trying to force them into actions contrary to their primeval instincts, but I could not believe that happiness was to be brought to them by a gospel of industrialism and forced labour.

Nevertheless, when morning came I resumed the interminable discussions of the materialistic conception of history and the merits of a truly popular government. Those with whom I discussed had not seen the sleeping wanderers, and would not have been interested if they had seen them, since they were not material for propaganda. But something of that patient silence had communicated itself to me, something lonely and unspoken remained in my heart throughout all the comfortable familiar intellectual talk. And at last I began to feel that all politics are inspired by a grinning devil, teaching the energetic and quickwitted to torture submissive populations for the profit of pocket or power or theory. As we journeyed on, fed by food extracted from the peasants, protected by an army recruited from among their sons, I wondered what we had to give them in return. But I found no answer. From time to time I heard their sad songs or the haunting music of the balalaika; but the sound mingled with the great silence of the steppes, and left me with a terrible questioning pain in which Occidental hopefulness grew pale.

It was in this mood that I set out for China to seek a new hope.

# 2

## CHINA BEFORE THE NINETEENTH CENTURY

Where the Chinese came from is a matter of conjecture. Their early history is known only from their own annals, which throw no light upon the question. The Shu-King, one of the Confucian classics (edited, not composed, by Confucius), begins, like Livy, with legendary accounts of princes whose virtues and vices are intended to supply edification or warning to subsequent rulers. Yao and Shun were two model Emperors, whose date (if any) was somewhere in the third millennium B.C. "The age of Yao and Shun," in Chinese literature, means what "the Golden Age" means with us. It seems certain that, when Chinese history begins, the Chinese occupied only a small part of what is now China, along the banks of the Yellow River. They were agricultural, and had already reached a fairly high level of civilization—much higher than that of any other part of Eastern Asia. The Yellow River is a fierce and terrible stream, too swift for navigation, turgid, and full of mud, depositing silt upon its bed until it rises above the surrounding country, when it suddenly alters its course, sweeping away villages and towns in a destructive torrent. Among most early agricultural nations, such a river would have inspired superstitious awe, and floods would have been averted by human sacrifice; in the Shu-King, however, there is little trace of superstition. Yao and Shun, and Yu (the latter's successor), were all occupied in combating the inundations, but their methods were those of the engineer, not of the miracle-worker. This shows, at least, the state of belief in the time of Confucius. The character ascribed to Yao shows what was expected of an Emperor:—

> He was reverential, intelligent, accomplished, and thoughtful— naturally and without effort. He was sincerely courteous, and capable of all complaisance. The display of these qualities reached to the four extremities of the empire, and extended from earth to heaven. He was able to make the able and virtuous distinguished, and thence proceeded to the love of the nine classes of his kindred, who all became harmonious. He also regulated and polished the people of his domain, who all became brightly intelligent. Finally, he united and harmonized the myriad States of the empire; and lo! the black-haired people were transformed. The result was universal concord.[1]

The first date which can be assigned with precision in Chinese history is that of an eclipse of the sun in 776 B.C.[2] There is no reason to doubt the general correctness of the records for considerably earlier times, but their exact chronology cannot be fixed. At this period, the Chou dynasty, which fell in 249 B.C. and is supposed to have begun in 1122 B.C., was already declining in power as compared with a number of nominally subordinate feudal States. The position of the Emperor at this time, and for the next 500 years, was similar to that of the King of France during those parts of the Middle Ages when his authority was at its lowest ebb. Chinese history consists of a series of dynasties, each strong at first and weak afterwards, each gradually losing control over subordinates, each followed by a period of anarchy (sometimes lasting for centuries), and ultimately succeeded by a new dynasty which temporarily re-establishes a strong Central Government. Historians always attribute the fall of a dynasty to the excessive power of eunuchs, but perhaps this is, in part, a literary convention.

What distinguishes the Emperor is not so much his political power, which fluctuates with the strength of his personality, as certain religious prerogatives. The Emperor is the Son of Heaven; he sacrifices to Heaven at the winter solstice. The early Chinese used "Heaven" as synonymous with "The Supreme Ruler," a monotheistic God;[3] indeed Professor Giles maintains, by arguments which seem conclusive, that the correct translation of the Emperor's title would be "Son of God." The word "Tien," in Chinese, is used both for the sky and for God, though the latter sense has become rare. The expression "Shang Ti," which means "Supreme Ruler," belongs in the main to pre-Confucian times, but both terms originally represented a God as definitely anthropomorphic as the God of the Old Testament.[4]

As time went by the Supreme Ruler became more shadowy, while "Heaven" remained, on account of the Imperial rites connected with it. The Emperor alone had the privilege of worshipping "Heaven," and the rites continued practically unchanged until the fall of the Manchu dynasty in 1911. In modern times they were performed in the Temple of Heaven Peking, one of the most beautiful places in the world. The animal sacrifice in the Temple of Heaven represented almost the sole official survival of pre-Confucian religion, or indeed of anything that could be called religion in the strict sense; for Buddhism and Taoism have never had any connection with the State.

The history of China is known in some detail from the year 722 B.C., because with this year begins Confucius' *Springs and Autumns*, which is a chronicle of the State of Lu, in which Confucius was an official.

One of the odd things about the history of China is that after the Emperors have been succeeding each other for more than 2,000 years, one comes to a ruler who is known as the "First Emperor," Shih Huang Ti. He acquired control over the whole Empire, after a series of wars, in 221 B.C., and died in 210 B.C. Apart from his conquests, he is remarkable for three achievements: the building of the Great Wall against the Huns, the destruction of feudalism, and the burning of the books. The destruction of feudalism, it must be confessed, had to be repeated by many subsequent rulers; for a long time, feudalism tended to grow up again whenever the Central Government was in weak hands. But Shih Huang Ti was the first ruler who made his authority really effective over all China in historical times. Although his dynasty came to an end with his son, the impression he made is shown by the fact that our word "China" is probably derived from his family name, Tsin or Chin[5]. (The Chinese put the family name first.) His Empire was roughly co-extensive with what is now China proper.

The destruction of the books was a curious incident. Shih Huang Ti, as appears from his calling himself "First Emperor," disliked being reminded of the fact that China had existed before his time; therefore history was anathema to him. Moreover the literati were already a strong force in the country, and were always (following Confucius) in favour of the preservation of ancient customs, whereas Shih Huang Ti was a vigorous innovator. Moreover, he appears to have been uneducated and not of pure Chinese race. Moved by the combined motives of vanity and radicalism, he issued an edict decreeing that—

> All official histories, except the memoirs of Tsin (his own family), shall be burned; except the persons who have the office of literati of the great learning, those who in the Empire permit themselves to hide the Shi-King, the Shu-King (Confucian classics), or the discourses of the hundred schools, must all go before the local civil and military authorities so that they may be burned. Those who shall dare to discuss among themselves the Shi-King and the Shu-King shall be put to death and their corpses exposed in a public place; those who shall make use of antiquity to belittle modern times shall be put to death with their relations. . . . Thirty days after the publication of this edict, those who have not burned their books shall be branded and sent to forced labour. The books which shall not be proscribed are those of medicine and pharmacy, of divination . . ., of agriculture and of arboriculture. As for those who desire to study the laws and ordinances, let them take the officials as masters. (Cordier, op. cit. i. p. 203.)

It will be seen that the First Emperor was something of a Bolshevik. The Chinese literati, naturally, have blackened his memory. On the other hand, modern Chinese reformers, who have experienced the opposition of old-fashioned scholars, have a certain sympathy with his attempt to destroy the innate conservatism of his subjects. Thus Li Ung Bing[6] says:—

No radical change can take place in China without encountering the opposition of the literati. This was no less the case then than it is now. To abolish feudalism by one stroke was a radical change indeed. Whether the change was for the better or the worse, the men of letters took no time to inquire; whatever was good enough for their fathers was good enough for them and their children. They found numerous authorities in the classics to support their contention and these they freely quoted to show that Shih Huang Ti was wrong. They continued to criticize the government to such an extent that something had to be done to silence the voice of antiquity. As to how far this decree (on the burning of the books) was enforced, it is hard to say. At any rate, it exempted all libraries of the government, or such as were in posses-sion of a class of officials called Po Szu or Learned Men. If any real damage was done to Chinese literature under the decree in question, it is safe to say that it was not of such a nature as later writers would have us believe. Still, this extreme measure failed to secure the desired end, and a number of the men of letters in Han Yang, the capital, was subsequently buried alive.

This passage is written from the point of view of Young China, which is anxious to assimilate Western learning in place of the dead scholar-ship of the Chinese classics. China, like every other civilized country, has a tradition which stands in the way of progress. The Chinese have excelled in stability rather than in progress; therefore Young China, which perceives that the advent of industrial civilization has made progress essential to continued national existence, naturally looks with a favourable eye upon Shih Huang Ti's struggle with the reactionary pedants of his age. The very considerable literature which has come down to us from before his time shows, in any case, that his edict was somewhat ineffective; and in fact it was repealed after twenty-two years, in 191 B.C.

After a brief reign by the son of the First Emperor, who did not inherit his capacity, we come to the great Han dynasty, which reigned from 206 B.C. to A.D. 220. This was the great age of Chinese imperialism—exactly coeval with the great age of Rome. In the course of their campaigns in Northern India and Central Asia, the Chinese were brought into contact with India, with Persia, and even with the Roman Empire.[7] Their relations with India had a profound effect upon their religion, as well as upon that of Japan, since they led to the introduction of Buddhism. Relations with Rome were chiefly promoted by the Roman desire for silk, and continued until the rise of Mohammedanism. They had little importance for China, though we learn, for example, that about A.D. 164 a treatise on astronomy was brought to China from the Roman Empire.[8] Marcus Aurelius appears in Chinese history under the name An Tun, which stands for Antoninus.

It was during this period that the Chinese acquired that immense prestige in the Far East which lasted until the arrival of European armies and navies in the nineteenth century. One is sometimes tempted to think that the irruption of the white man into China may prove almost as ephemeral as the raids of Huns and Tartars into Europe. The military superiority of Europe to Asia is not an eternal law of nature, as we are tempted to think; and our superiority in civilization is a mere delusion. Our histories, which treat the Mediterranean as the centre of the universe, give quite a wrong perspective. Cordier,[9] dealing with the campaigns and voyages of discovery which took place under the Han dynasty, says:—

> The Occidentals have singularly contracted the field of the history of the world when they have grouped around the people of Israel, Greece, and Rome the little that they knew of the expansion of the human race, being completely ignorant of these voyagers who ploughed the China Sea and the Indian Ocean, of these cavalcades across the immensities of Central Asia up to the Persian Gulf. The greatest part of the

universe, and at the same time a civilization different but certainly as
developed as that of the ancient Greeks and Romans, remained unknown to those who wrote the history of their little world while they
believed that they were setting forth the history of the world as a whole.

In our day, this provincialism, which impregnates all our culture, is
liable to have disastrous consequences politically, as well as for the
civilization of mankind. We must make room for Asia in our thoughts,
if we are not to rouse Asia to a fury of self-assertion.

After the Han dynasty there are various short dynasties and periods
of disorder, until we come to the Tang dynasty (A.D. 618–907). Under
this dynasty, in its prosperous days, the Empire acquired its greatest
extent, and art and poetry reached their highest point.[10] The Empire of
Jenghis Khan (died 1227) was considerably greater, and contained a
great part of China; but Jenghis Khan was a foreign conqueror. Jenghis
and his generals, starting from Mongolia, appeared as conquerors in
China, India, Persia, and Russia. Throughout Central Asia, Jenghis destroyed every man, woman, and child in the cities he captured. When
Merv was captured, it was transformed into a desert and 700,000 people were killed. But it was said that many had escaped by lying among
the corpses and pretending to be dead; therefore at the capture of Nis-
hapur, shortly afterwards, it was ordered that all the inhabitants should
have their heads cut off. Three pyramids of heads were made, one of
men, one of women, and one of children. As it was feared that some
might have escaped by hiding underground, a detachment of soldiers
was left to kill any that might emerge.[11] Similar horrors were enacted
at Moscow and Kieff, in Hungary and Poland. Yet the man responsible
for these massacres was sought in alliance by St. Louis and the Pope.
The times of Jenghis Khan remind one of the present day, except that
his methods of causing death were more merciful than those that have
been employed since the Armistice.

Kublai Khan (died 1294), who is familiar, at least by name, through
Marco Polo and Coleridge, was the grandson of Jenghis Khan, and the
first Mongol who was acknowledged Emperor of China, where he
ousted the Sung dynasty (960–1277). By this time, contact with China

had somewhat abated the savagery of the first conquerors. Kublai removed his capital from Kara Korum in Mongolia to Peking. He built walls like those which still surround the city, and established on the walls an observatory which is preserved to this day. Until 1900, two of the astronomical instruments constructed by Kublai were still to be seen in this observatory, but the Germans removed them to Potsdam after the suppression of the Boxers.[12] I understand they have been restored in accordance with one of the provisions of the Treaty of Versailles. If so, this was probably the most important benefit which that treaty secured to the world.

Kublai plays the same part in Japanese history that Philip II plays in the history of England. He prepared an Invincible Armada, or rather two successive armadas, to conquer Japan, but they were defeated, partly by storms, and partly by Japanese valour.

After Kublai, the Mongol Emperors more and more adopted Chinese ways, and lost their tyrannical vigour. Their dynasty came to an end in 1370, and was succeeded by the pure Chinese Ming dynasty, which lasted until the Manchu conquest of 1644. The Manchus in turn adopted Chinese ways, and were overthrown by a patriotic revolution in 1911, having contributed nothing notable to the native culture of China except the pigtail, officially abandoned at the Revolution.

The persistence of the Chinese Empire down to our own day is not to be attributed to any military skill; on the contrary, considering its extent and resources, it has at most times shown itself weak and incompetent in war. Its southern neighbours were even less warlike, and were less in extent. Its northern and western neighbours inhabited a barren country, largely desert, which was only capable of supporting a very sparse population. The Huns were defeated by the Chinese after centuries of warfare; the Tartars and Manchus, on the contrary, conquered China. But they were too few and too uncivilized to impose their ideas or their way of life upon China, which absorbed them and went on its way as if they had never existed. Rome could have survived the Goths, if they had come alone, but the successive waves of barbarians came too quickly to be all civilized in turn. China was saved from this fate by the Gobi Desert and the Tibetan uplands. Since the white men have taken to coming by sea, the old geographical immunity is lost, and greater energy will be required to preserve the national independence.

In spite of geographical advantages, however, the persistence of Chinese civilization, fundamentally unchanged since the introduction of Buddhism, is a remarkable phenomenon. Egypt and Babylonia persisted as long, but since they fell there has been nothing comparable in the world. Perhaps the main cause is the immense population of China, with an almost complete identity of culture throughout. In the middle of the eighth century, the population of China is estimated at over 50 millions, though ten years later, as a result of devastating wars, it is said to have sunk to about 17 millions.[13] A census has been taken at various times in Chinese history, but usually a census of houses, not of individuals. From the number of houses the population is computed by a more or less doubtful calculation. It is probable, also, that different methods were adopted on different occasions, and that comparisons between different enumerations are therefore rather unsafe. Putnam Weale[14] says:—

The first census taken by the Manchus in 1651, after the restoration of order, returned China's population at 55 million persons, which is less than the number given in the first census of the Han dynasty, A.D. 1, and about the same as when Kublai Khan established the Mongal dynasty in 1295. (This is presumably a misprint, as Kublai died in 1294.) Thus we are faced by the amazing fact that, from the beginning of the Christian era, the toll of life taken by internecine and frontier wars in China was so great that in spite of all territorial expansion the population for upwards of sixteen centuries remained more or less stationary. There is in all history no similar record. Now, however, came a vast change. Thus three years after the death of the celebrated Manchu Emperor Kang Hsi, in 1720, the population had risen to 125 millions. At the beginning of the reign of the no less illustrious Ch'ien Lung (1743) it was returned at 145 millions; towards the end of his reign, in 1783, it had doubled, and was given as 283 millions. In the reign of Chia Ch'ing (1812) it had risen to 360 millions; before the Taiping rebellion (1842) it had grown to 413 millions; after that terrible rising it sunk to 261 millions.

I do not think such definite statements are warranted. The *China Year Book* for 1919 (the latest I have seen) says (p. 1):—

The taking of a census by the methods adopted in Western nations has never yet been attempted in China, and consequently estimates of the total population have varied to an extraordinary degree. The nearest approach to a reliable estimate is, probably, the census taken by the Minchengpu (Ministry of Interior) in 1910, the results of which are embodied in a report submitted to the Department of State at Washington by Mr. Raymond P. Tenney, a Student Interpreter at the U.S. Legation, Peking.... It is pointed out that even this census can only be regarded as approximate, as, with few exceptions, households and not individuals were counted.

The estimated population of the Chinese Empire (exclusive of Tibet) is given, on the basis of this census, as 329,542,000, while the population of Tibet is estimated at 1,500,000. Estimates which have been made at various other dates are given as follows (p. 2):—

| A.D. | | A.D. | |
|---|---|---|---|
| 1381 | 59,850,000 | 1760 | { 143,125,225 |
| 1412 | 65,377,000 | | { 203,916,477 |
| 1580 | 60,692,000 | 1761 | 205,293,053 |
| 1662 | 21,068,000 | 1762 | 198,214,553 |
| 1668 | 25,386,209 | 1790 | 155,249,897 |
| 1710 | { 23,312,200 | 1792 | { 307,467,200 |
| | { 27,241,129 | | { 333,000,000 |
| 1711 | 28,241,129 | 1812 | { 362,467,183 |
| 1736 | 125,046,245 | | { 360,440,000 |
| 1743 | { 157,343,975 | 1842 | 413,021,000 |
| | { 149,332,730 | 1868 | 404,946,514 |
| | { 150,265,475 | 1881 | 380,000,000 |
| 1753 | 103,050,600 | 1882 | 381,309,000 |
| | | 1885 | 377,636,000 |

These figures suffice to show how little is known about the population of China. Not only are widely divergent estimates made in the same year (*e.g.* 1760), but in other respects the figures are incredible. Mr. Putnam Weale might contend that the drop from 60 millions in 1580 to 21 millions in 1662 was due to the wars leading to the Manchu conquest. But no one can believe that between 1711 and 1736 the population increased from 28 millions to 125 millions, or that it doubled between 1790 and 1792. No one knows whether the population of China is increasing or diminishing, whether people in general have large or small families, or any of the other facts that vital statistics are designed to elucidate. What is said on these subjects, however dogmatic, is no more than guess-work. Even the population of Peking is unknown. It is said to be about 900,000, but it may be anywhere between 800,000 and a million. As for the population of the Chinese Empire, it is probably safe to assume that it is between three and four hundred millions, and somewhat likely that it is below three hundred and fifty millions. Very little indeed can be said with confidence as to the population of China in former times; so little that, on the whole, authors who give statistics are to be distrusted.

There are certain broad features of the traditional Chinese civilization which give it its distinctive character. I should be inclined to select as the most important: (1) The use of ideograms instead of an alphabet in writing; (2) The substitution of the Confucian ethic for religion among the educated classes; (3) government by literati chosen by examination instead of by a hereditary aristocracy. The family system distinguishes traditional China from modern Europe, but represents a stage which most other civilizations have passed through, and which is therefore not distinctively Chinese; the three characteristics which I have enumerated, on the other hand, distinguish China from all other countries of past times. Something must be said at this stage about each of the three.

1. As everyone knows, the Chinese do not have letters, as we do, but symbols for whole words. This has, of course, many inconveniences: it means that, in learning to write, there are an immense number of different signs to be learnt, not only 26 as with us; that

there is no such thing as alphabetical order, so that dictionaries, files, catalogues, etc., are difficult to arrange and linotype is impossible; that foreign words, such as proper names and scientific terms, cannot be written down by sound, as in European languages, but have to be represented by some elaborate device.[15] For these reasons, there is a movement for phonetic writing among the more advanced Chinese reformers; and I think the success of this movement is essential if China is to take her place among the bustling hustling nations which consider that they have a monopoly of all excellence. Even if there were no other argument for the change, the difficulty of elementary education, where reading and writing take so long to learn, would be alone sufficient to decide any believer in democracy. For practical purposes, therefore, the movement for phonetic writing deserves support.

There are, however, many considerations, less obvious to a European, which can be adduced in favour of the ideographic system, to which something of the solid stability of the Chinese civilization is probably traceable. To us, it seems obvious that a written word must represent a sound, whereas to the Chinese it represents an idea. We have adopted the Chinese system ourselves as regards numerals; "1922," for example, can be read in English, French, or any other language, with quite different sounds. Similarly what is written in Chinese characters can be read throughout China, in spite of the difference of dialects which are mutually unintelligible when spoken. Even a Japanese, without knowing a word of spoken Chinese, can read out Chinese script in Japanese, just as he could read a row of numerals written by an English-man. And the Chinese can still read their classics, although the spoken language must have changed as much as French has changed from Latin.

The advantage of writing over speech is its greater permanence, which enables it to be a means of communication between different places and different times. But since the spoken language changes from place to place and from time to time, the characteristic advantage of writing is more fully attained by a script which does not aim at representing spoken sounds than by one which does.

Speaking historically, there is nothing peculiar in the Chinese method of writing, which represents a stage through which all writing probably passed. Writing everywhere seems to have begun as pictures, not as a symbolic representation of sounds. I understand that in Egyptian hieroglyphics the course of development from ideograms to phonetic writing can be studied. What is peculiar in China is the preservation of the ideographic system throughout thousands of years of advanced civilization—a preservation probably due, at least in part, to the fact that the spoken language is monosyllabic, uninflected and full of homonyms.

As to the way in which the Chinese system of writing has affected the mentality of those who employ it, I find some suggestive reflections in an article published in the *Chinese Students' Monthly* (Baltimore), for February 1922, by Mr. Chi Li, in an article on "Some Anthropological Problems of China." He says (p. 327):—

Language has been traditionally treated by European scientists as a collection of sounds instead of an expression of something inner and deeper than the vocal apparatus as it should be. The accumulative effect of language-symbols upon one's mental formulation is still an unexploited field. Dividing the world culture of the living races on this basis, one perceives a fundamental difference of its types between the alphabetical users and the hieroglyphic users, each of which has its own virtues and vices. Now, with all respects to alphabetical civilization, it must be frankly stated that it has a grave and inherent defect in its lack of solidity. The most civilized portion under the alphabetical culture is also inhabited by the most fickled people. The history of the Western land repeats the same story over and over again. Thus up and down with the Greeks; up and down with Rome; up and down with the Arabs. The ancient Semitic and Hametic peoples are essentially alphabetic users, and their civilizations show the same lack of solidity as the Greeks and the Romans. Certainly this phenomenon can be partially explained by the extra-fluidity of the alphabetical language which cannot be depended upon as a suitable organ to conserve any solid idea. Intellectual contents of these people may be likened to waterfalls and cataracts, rather than seas and oceans. No other people is richer in ideas than they; but no people would give up their valuable ideas as quickly as they do. . . .

The Chinese language is by all means the counterpart of the alphabetic stock. It lacks most of the virtues that are found in the alphabetic language; but as an embodiment of simple and final truth, it is invulnerable to storm and stress. It has already protected the Chinese civilization for more than forty centuries. It is solid, square, and beautiful, exactly as the spirit of it represents. Whether it is the spirit that has produced this language or whether this language has in turn accentuated the spirit remains to be determined.

Without committing ourselves wholly to the theory here set forth, which is impregnated with Chinese patriotism, we must nevertheless admit that the Westerner is unaccustomed to the idea of "alphabetical civilization" as merely one kind, to which he happens to belong. I am not competent to judge as to the importance of the ideographic script in producing the distinctive characteristics of Chinese civilization, but I have no doubt that this importance is very great, and is more or less of the kind indicated in the above quotation.

2. Confucius (B.C. 551–479) must be reckoned, as regards his social influence, with the founders of religions. His effect on institutions and on men's thoughts has been of the same kind of magnitude as that of Buddha, Christ, or Mahomet, but curiously different in its nature. Unlike Buddha and Christ, he is a completely historical character, about whose life a great deal is known, and with whom legend and myth have been less busy than with most men of his kind. What most distinguishes him from other founders is that he inculcated a strict code of ethics, which has been respected ever since, but associated it with very little religious dogma, which gave place to complete theological scepticism in the countless generations of Chinese literati who revered his memory and administered the Empire.

Confucius himself belongs rather to the type of Lycurgus and Solon than to that of the great founders of religions. He was a practical statesman, concerned with the administration of the State; the virtues he sought to inculcate were not those of personal holiness, or designed to secure salvation in a future life, but rather those which lead to a peaceful and prosperous community here on earth. His outlook was essentially conservative, and aimed at preserving the virtues of former ages. He accepted the existing religion—a rather unemphatic monotheism, combined with belief that the spirits of the dead preserved a shadowy existence, which it was the duty of their descendants to render as comfortable as possible. He did not, however, lay any stress upon supernatural matters. In answer to a question, he gave the following definition of wisdom: "To cultivate earnestly our duty towards our neighbour, and to reverence spiritual beings while maintaining always a due reserve."[16] But reverence for spiritual beings was not an *active* part of Confucianism, except in the form of ancestor-worship, which was part of filial piety, and thus merged in duty towards one's neighbour. Filial piety included obedience to the Emperor, except when he was so wicked as to forfeit his divine right—for the Chinese, unlike the Japanese, have always held that resistance to the Emperor was justified if he governed very badly. The following passage from Professor Giles[17] illustrates this point:—

> The Emperor has been uniformly regarded as the son of God by adoption only, and liable to be displaced from that position as a punishment for the offence of misrule.... If the ruler failed in his duties, the obligation of the people was at an end, and his divine right disappeared simultaneously. Of this we have an example in a portion of the Canon to be examined by and by. Under the year 558 B.C. we find the following narrative. One of the feudal princes asked an official, saying, "Have not the people of the Wei State done very wrong in expelling their ruler?" "Perhaps the ruler himself," was the reply, "may have done very wrong. . . . If the life of the people is impoverished, and if the spirits are deprived of their sacrifices, of what use is the ruler, and what can the people do but get rid of him?"

This very sensible doctrine has been accepted at all times throughout Chinese history, and has made rebellions only too frequent.

Filial piety, and the strength of the family generally, are perhaps the weakest point in Confucian ethics, the only point where the system departs seriously from common sense. Family feeling has militated against public spirit, and the authority of the old has increased the tyranny of ancient custom. In the present day, when China is confronted with problems requiring a radically new outlook, these features of the Confucian system have made it a barrier to necessary reconstruction, and accordingly we find all those foreigners who wish to exploit China praising the old tradition and deriding the efforts of Young China to construct something more suited to modern needs. The way in which Confucian emphasis on filial piety prevented the growth of public spirit is illustrated by the following story:[18]

> One of the feudal princes was boasting to Confucius of the high level of morality which prevailed in his own State. "Among us here," he said, "you will find upright men. If a father has stolen a sheep, his son will give evidence against him." "In my part of the country," replied Confucius, "there is a different standard from this. A father will shield his son, a son will shield his father. It is thus that uprightness will be found."

It is interesting to contrast this story with that of the elder Brutus and his sons, upon which we in the West were all brought up.

Chao Ki, expounding the Confucian doctrine, says it is contrary to filial piety to refuse a lucrative post by which to relieve the indigence of one's aged parents.[19] This form of sin, however, is rare in China as in other countries.

The worst failure of filial piety, however, is to remain without children, since ancestors are supposed to suffer if they have no descendants to keep up their cult. It is probable that this doctrine has made the Chinese more prolific, in which case it has had great biological importance. Filial piety is, of course, in no way peculiar to China, but has been universal at a certain stage of culture. In this respect, as in certain others, what is peculiar to China is the preservation of the old custom after a very high level of civilization had been attained. The early Greeks and Romans did not differ from the Chinese in this respect, but as their civilization advanced the family became less and less important. In China, this did not begin to happen until our own day.

Whatever may be said against filial piety carried to excess, it is certainly less harmful than its Western counterpart, patriotism. Both, of course, err in inculcating duties to a certain portion of mankind to the practical exclusion of the rest. But patriotism directs one's loyalty to a fighting unit, which filial piety does not (except in a very primitive society). Therefore patriotism leads much more easily to militarism and imperialism. The principal method of advancing the interests of one's nation is homicide; the principal method of advancing the interest of one's family is corruption and intrigue. Therefore family feeling is less harmful than patriotism. This view is borne out by the history and present condition of China as compared to Europe.

Apart from filial piety, Confucianism was, in practice, mainly a code of civilized behaviour, degenerating at times into an etiquette book. It taught self-restraint, moderation, and above all courtesy. Its moral code was not, like those of Buddhism and Christianity, so severe that only a few saints could hope to live up to it, or so much concerned with personal salvation as to be incompatible with political institutions. It was not difficult for a man of the world to live up to the more imperative parts of the Confucian teaching. But in order to do this he must exercise at all times a certain kind of self-control—an extension of the kind which children learn when they are taught to "behave." He must not break into violent passions; he must not be arrogant; he must "save face," and never inflict humiliations upon defeated adversaries; he must be moderate in all things, never carried away by excessive love or hate; in a word, he must keep calm reason always in control of all his actions. This attitude existed in Europe in the eighteenth century, but perished in the French Revolution: romanticism, Rousseau, and the guillotine put an end to it. In China, though wars and revolutions have occurred constantly, Confucian calm has survived them all, making them less terrible for the participants, and making all who were not immediately involved hold aloof. It is bad manners in China to attack your adversary in wet weather. Wu-Pei-Fu, I am told, once did it, and won a victory; the beaten general complained of the breach of etiquette; so Wu-Pei-Fu went back to the position he held before the battle, and fought all over again on a fine day. (It should be said that battles in China are seldom bloody.) In such a country, militarism is not the scourge it is with us; and the difference is due to the Confucian ethics.[20]

Confucianism did not assume its present form until the twelfth century A.D., when the personal God in whom Confucius had believed was thrust aside by the philosopher Chu Fu Tze,[21] whose interpretation of Confucianism has ever since been recognized as orthodox. Since the fall of the Mongols (1370), the Government has uniformly favoured Confucianism as the teaching of the State; before that, there were struggles with Buddhism and Taoism, which were connected with magic, and appealed to superstitious Emperors, quite a number of whom died of drinking the Taoist elixir of life. The Mongol Emperors were Buddhists of the Lama religion, which still prevails in Tibet and Mongolia; but the Manchu Emperors, though also northern conquerors, were ultra-orthodox Confucians. It has been customary in China, for many centuries, for the literati to be pure Confucians, sceptical in religion but not in morals, while the rest of the population believed and practised all three religions simultaneously. The Chinese have not the belief, which we owe to the Jews, that if one religion is true, all others must be false. At the present day, however, there appears to be very little in the way of religion in China, though the belief in magic lingers on among the uneducated. At all times, even when there was religion, its intensity was far less than in Europe. It is remarkable that religious scepticism has not led, in China, to any corresponding ethical scepticism, as it has done repeatedly in Europe.

3. I come now to the system of selecting officials by competitive examination, without which it is hardly likely that so literary and unsuperstitious a system as that of Confucius could have maintained its hold. The view of the modern Chinese on this subject is set forth by

the present President of the Republic of China, Hsu Shi-chang, in his book on China after the War, pp. 59–60.[22] After considering the educational system under the Chou dynasty, he continues:

> In later periods, in spite of minor changes, the importance of moral virtues continued to be stressed upon. For instance, during the most flourishing period of Tang Dynasty (627–650 A.D.), the Imperial Academy of Learning, known as Kuo-tzu-chien, was composed of four collegiate departments, in which ethics was considered as the most important of all studies. It was said that in the Academy there were more than three thousand students who were able and virtuous in nearly all respects, while the total enrolment, including aspirants from Korea and Japan, was as high as eight thousand. At the same time, there was a system of "elections" through which able and virtuous men were recommended by different districts to the Emperor for appointment to public offices. College training and local elections supplemented each other, but in both moral virtues were given the greatest emphasis.
>
> Although the Imperial Academy exists till this day, it has never been as flourishing as during that period. For this change the introduction of the competitive examination or Ko-chü system, must be held responsible. The "election" system furnished no fixed standard for the recommendation of public service candidates, and, as a result, tended to create an aristocratic class from which alone were to be found eligible men. Consequently, the Sung Emperors (960–1277 A.D.) abolished the elections, set aside the Imperial Academy, and inaugurated the competitive examination system in their place. The examinations were to supply both scholars and practical statesmen, and they were periodically held throughout the later dynasties until the introduction of the modern educational regime. Useless and stereotyped as they were in later days, they once served some useful purpose. Besides, the ethical background of Chinese education had already been so firmly established, that, in spite of the emphasis laid by these examinations on pure literary attainments, moral teachings have survived till this day in family education and in private schools.

Although the system of awarding Government posts for proficiency in examinations is much better than most other systems that have prevailed, such as nepotism, bribery, threats of insurrection, etc., yet the Chinese system, at any rate after it assumed its final form, was harmful through the fact that it was based solely on the classics, that it was purely literary, and that it allowed no scope whatever for originality. The system was established in its final form by the Emperor Hung Wu (1368–1398), and remained unchanged until 1905. One of the first objects of modern Chinese reformers was to get it swept away. Li Ung Bing[23] says:

> In spite of the many good things that may be said to the credit of Hung Wu, he will ever be remembered in connection with a form of evil which has eaten into the very heart of the nation. This was the system of triennial examinations, or rather the form of Chinese composition, called the "Essay," or the "Eight Legs," which, for the first time in the history of Chinese literature, was made the basis of all literary contests. It was so-named, because after the introduction of the theme the writer was required to treat it in four paragraphs, each consisting of two members, made up of an equal number of sentences and words. The theme was always chosen from either the Four Books, or the Five Classics. The writer could not express any opinion of his own, or any views at variance with those expressed by Chu Hsi and his school. All he was required to do was to put the few words of Confucius, or whomsoever it might be, into an essay in conformity with the prescribed rules. Degrees, which were to serve as passports to Government positions, were awarded [to] the best writers. To say that the training afforded by the time required to make a man efficient in the art of such writing, would at the same time qualify him to hold the various offices under the Government, was absurd. But absurd as the whole system was, it was handed down to recent times from the third year of the reign of Hung Wu, and was not abolished until a few years ago. No system was more perfect or effective in retarding the intellectual and literary development of a nation. With her "Eight Legs," China long ago reached the lowest point on her downhill journey. It is largely

on account of the long lease of life that was granted to this rotten system that the teachings of the Sung philosophers have been so long venerated.

These are the words of a Chinese patriot of the present day, and no doubt, as a modern system, the "Eight Legs" deserve all the hard things that he says about them. But in the fourteenth century, when one considers the practicable alternatives, one can see that there was probably much to be said for such a plan. At any rate, for good or evil, the examination system profoundly affected the civilization of China. Among its good effects were: A widely-diffused respect for learning; the possibility of doing without a hereditary aristocracy; the selection of administrators who must at least have been capable of industry; and the preservation of Chinese civilization in spite of barbarian conquest. But, like so much else in traditional China, it has had to be swept away to meet modern needs. I hope nothing of greater value will have to perish in the struggle to repel the foreign exploiters and the fierce and cruel system which they miscall civilization.

## NOTES

1   Legge's *Shu-King*, p. 15. Quoted in Hirth, *Ancient History of China,* Columbia University Press, 1911—a book which gives much useful critical information about early China.
2   Hirth, op. cit. p. 174. 775 is often wrongly given.
3   See Hirth, op. cit., p. 100 ff.
4   On this subject, see Professor Giles's *Confucianism and its Rivals,* Williams & Norgate, 1915, Lecture I, especially p. 9.
5   Cf. Henri Cordier, *Histoire Générale de la Chine,* Paris, 1920, vol. i. p. 213.
6   *Outlines of Chinese History* (Shanghai, Commercial Press, 1914), p. 61.
7   See Hirth, *China and the Roman Orient* (Leipzig and Shanghai, 1885), an admirable and fascinating monograph. There are allusions to the Chinese in Virgil and Horace; cf. Cordier, op. cit., i. p. 271.
8   Cordier, op. cit. i. p. 281.
9   Cordier, op. cit. i. p. 237.
10  Murdoch, in his *History of Japan* (vol. i. p. 146), thus describes the greatness of the early Tang Empire:
    "In the following year (618) Li Yuen, Prince of T'ang, established the illustrious dynasty of that name, which continued to sway the fortunes of China for

nearly three centuries (618–908). After a brilliant reign of ten years he handed over the imperial dignity to his son, Tai-tsung (627–650), perhaps the greatest monarch the Middle Kingdom has ever seen. At this time China undoubtedly stood in the very forefront of civilization. She was then the most powerful, the most enlightened, the most progressive, and the best governed empire, not only in Asia, but on the face of the globe. Tai-tsung's frontiers reached from the confines of Persia, the Caspian Sea, and the Altai of the Kirghis steppe, along these mountains to the north side of the Gobi desert eastward to the inner Hing-an, while Sogdiana, Khorassan, and the regions around the Hindu Kush also acknowledged his suzerainty. The sovereign of Nepal and Magadha in India sent envoys; and in 643 envoys appeared from the Byzantine Empire and the Court of Persia."

11   Cordier, op. cit. ii. p. 212.

12   Cordier, op. cit. ii. p. 339.

13   Cordier, op. cit. i. p. 484.

14   *The Truth About China and Japan.* George Allen & Unwin, Ltd., pp. 13, 14.

15   For example, the nearest approach that could be made in Chinese to my own name was "Lo-Su." There is a word "Lo," and a word "Su," for both of which there are characters; but no combination of characters gives a better approximation to the sound of my name.

16   Giles, op. cit., p. 74. Professor Giles adds, *à propos* of the phrase "maintaining always a due reserve," the following footnote: "Dr. Legge has ' to keep aloof from them,' which would be equivalent to 'have nothing to do with them.' Confucius seems rather to have meant ' no familiarity. '"

17   Op. cit., p. 21.

18   Giles, op. cit. p. 86.

19   Cordier, op. cit. i. p. 167.

20   As far as anti-militarism is concerned, Taoism is even more emphatic. "The best soldiers," says Lao-Tze, "do not fight." (Giles, op. cit. p. 150.) Chinese armies contain many good soldiers.

21   Giles, op. cit., Lecture VIII. When Chu Fu Tze was dead, and his son-in-law was watching beside his coffin, a singular incident occurred. Although the sage had spent his life teaching that miracles are impossible, the coffin rose and remained suspended three feet above the ground. The pious son-in-law was horrified. "O my revered father-in-law," he prayed, "do not destroy my faith that miracles are impossible." Whereupon the coffin slowly descended to earth again, and the son-in-law's faith revived.

22   Translated by the Bureau of Economic Information, Peking, 1920.

23   Op. cit. p. 233.

# 3

## CHINA AND THE WESTERN POWERS

In order to understand the international position of China, some facts concerning its nineteenth-century history are indispensable. China was for many ages the supreme empire of the Far East, embracing a vast and fertile area, inhabited by an industrious and civilized people. Aristocracy, in our sense of the word, came to an end before the beginning of the Christian era, and government was in the hands of officials chosen for their proficiency in writing in a dead language, as in England. Intercourse with the West was spasmodic and chiefly religious. In the early centuries of the Christian era, Buddhism was imported from India, and some Chinese scholars penetrated to that country to master the theology of the new religion in its native home, but in later times the intervening barbarians made the journey practically impossible. Nestorian Christianity reached China in the seventh century, and had a good deal of influence, but died out again. (What is known on this subject is chiefly from the Nestorian monument discovered in

Hsianfu in 1625.) In the seventeenth and early eighteenth centuries Roman Catholic missionaries acquired considerable favour at Court, because of their astronomical knowledge and their help in rectifying the irregularities and confusions of the Chinese calendar.[1] Their globes and astrolabes are still to be seen on the walls of Peking. But in the long run they could not resist quarrels between different orders, and were almost completely excluded from both China and Japan.

In the year 1793, a British ambassador, Lord Macartney, arrived in China, to request further trade facilities and the establishment of a permanent British diplomatic representative. The Emperor at this time was Chien Lung, the best of the Manchu dynasty, a cultivated man, a patron of the arts, and an exquisite calligraphist. (One finds specimens of his writing in all sorts of places in China.) His reply to King George III is given by Backhouse and Bland.[2] I wish I could quote it all, but some extracts must suffice. It begins:

> You, O King, live beyond the confines of many seas, nevertheless, impelled by your humble desire to partake of the benefits of our civilization, you have despatched a mission respectfully bearing your memorial. ... To show your devotion, you have also sent offerings of your country's produce. I have read your memorial: the earnest terms in which it is cast reveal a respectful humility on your part, which is highly praiseworthy.

He goes on to explain, with the patient manner appropriate in dealing with an importunate child, why George III's desires cannot possibly be gratified. An ambassador, he assures him, would be useless, for:

> If you assert that your reverence for our Celestial Dynasty fills you with a desire to acquire our civilization, our ceremonies and code of laws differ so completely from your own that, even if your Envoy were able to acquire the rudiments of our civilization, you could not possibly transplant our manners and customs to your alien soil. Therefore, however adept the Envoy might become, nothing would be gained thereby.

> Swaying the wide world, I have but one aim in view, namely, to main-
> tain a perfect governance and to fulfil the duties of the State; strange
> and costly objects do not interest me. I . . . have no use for your coun-
> try's manufactures. . . . It behoves you, O King, to respect my senti-
> ments and to display even greater devotion and loyalty in future, so
> that, by perpetual submission to our Throne, you may secure peace
> and prosperity for your country hereafter.

He can understand the English desiring the produce of China, but feels
that they have nothing worth having to offer in exchange:

"Our Celestial Empire possesses all things in prolific abundance
and lacks no product within its own borders. There was therefore no
need to import the manufactures of outside barbarians in exchange
for our own produce. But as the tea, silk and porcelain which the
Celestial Empire produces are absolute necessities to European nations
and to yourselves," the limited trade hitherto permitted at Canton is
to continue.

He would have shown less favour to Lord Macartney, but "I do not
forget the lonely remoteness of your island, cut off from the world by
intervening wastes of sea, nor do I overlook your excusable ignorance
of the usages of our Celestial Empire." He concludes with the injunc-
tion: "Tremblingly obey and show no negligence!"

What I want to suggest is that no one understands China until this
document has ceased to seem absurd. The Romans claimed to rule the
world, and what lay outside their Empire was to them of no account.
The Empire of Chien Lung was more extensive, with probably a larger
population; it had risen to greatness at the same time as Rome, and
had not fallen, but invariably defeated all its enemies, either by war or
by absorption. Its neighbours were comparatively barbarous, except
the Japanese, who acquired their civilization by slavish imitation of
China. The view of Chien Lung was no more absurd than that of Al-
exander the Great, sighing for new worlds to conquer when he had
never even heard of China, where Confucius had been dead already for
a hundred and fifty years. Nor was he mistaken as regards trade: China
produces everything needed for the happiness of its inhabitants, and

we have forced trade upon them solely for our benefit, giving them in exchange only things which they would do better without.

Unfortunately for China, its culture was deficient in one respect, namely science. In art and literature, in manners and customs, it was at least the equal of Europe; at the time of the Renaissance, Europe would not have been in any way the superior of the Celestial Empire. There is a museum in Peking where, side by side with good Chinese art, may be seen the presents which Louis XIV made to the Emperor when he wished to impress him with the splendour of *Le Roi Soleil*. Compared to the Chinese things surrounding them, they are tawdry and barbaric. The fact that Britain has produced Shakespeare and Milton, Locke and Hume, and all the other men who have adorned literature and the arts, does not make us superior to the Chinese. What makes us superior is Newton and Robert Boyle and their scientific successors. They make us superior by giving us greater proficiency in the art of killing. It is easier for an Englishman to kill a Chinaman than for a Chinaman to kill an Englishman. Therefore our civilization is superior to that of China, and Chien Lung is absurd. When we had finished with Napoleon, we soon set to work to demonstrate this proposition.

Our first war with China was in 1840, and was fought because the Chinese Government endeavoured to stop the importation of opium. It ended with the cession of Hong-Kong and the opening of five ports to British trade, as well as (soon afterwards) to the trade of France, America and Scandinavia. In 1856–60, the English and French jointly made war on China, and destroyed the Summer Palace near Peking,[3] a building whose artistic value, on account of the treasures it contained, must have been about equal to that of Saint Mark's in Venice and much greater than that of Rheims Cathedral. This act did much to persuade the Chinese of the superiority of our civilization, so they opened seven more ports and the river Yangtze, paid an indemnity and granted us more territory at Hong-Kong. In 1870, the Chinese were rash enough to murder a British diplomat, so the remaining British diplomats demanded and obtained an indemnity, five more ports, and a fixed tariff for opium. Next, the French took Annam and the British took Burma, both formerly under Chinese suzerainty. Then came the war with Japan in 1894–5, leading to Japan's complete victory and conquest of Korea. Japan's acquisitions would have been much greater but for the intervention of France, Germany and Russia, England holding aloof. This was the beginning of our support of Japan, inspired by fear of Russia. It also led to an alliance between China and Russia, as a reward for which Russia acquired all the important rights in Manchuria, which passed to Japan, partly after the Russo-Japanese war, and partly after the Bolshevik revolution.

The next incident begins with the murder of two German missionaries in Shantung in 1897. Nothing in their life became them like the leaving of it; for if they had lived they would probably have made very few converts, whereas by dying they afforded the world an object-lesson in Christian ethics. The Germans seized Kiaochow Bay and created a naval base there; they also acquired railway and mining rights in Shantung, which, by the Treaty of Versailles, passed to Japan in accordance with the Fourteen Points. Shantung therefore became virtually a Japanese possession, though America at Washington has insisted upon its restitution. The services of the two missionaries to civilization did not, however, end in China, for their death was constantly used in the German Reichstag during the first debates on the German Big Navy Bills, since it was held that warships would make Germany respected in China. Thus they helped to exacerbate the relations of England and Germany and to hasten the advent of the Great War. They also helped to bring on the Boxer rising, which is said to have begun as a movement against the Germans in Shantung, though the other Powers emulated the Germans in every respect, the Russians by creating a naval base at Port Arthur, the British by acquiring Wei-hai-wei and a sphere of influence in the Yangtze, and so on. The Americans alone held aloof, proclaiming the policy of Chinese integrity and the Open Door.

The Boxer rising is one of the few Chinese events that all Europeans know about. After we had demonstrated our superior virtue by the sack of Peking, we exacted a huge indemnity, and turned the Legation Quarter of Peking into a fortified city. To this day, it is enclosed by a wall, filled with European, American and Japanese troops, and surrounded by a bare space on which the Chinese are not allowed to build. It is administered by the diplomatic body, and the Chinese authorities have no powers over anyone within its gates. When some unusually corrupt and traitorous Government is overthrown, its members take refuge in the Japanese (or other) Legation and so escape the punishment of their crimes, while within the sacred precincts of the Legation Quarter the Americans erect a vast wireless station said to be capable of communicating directly with the United States. And so the refutation of Chien Lung is completed.

Out of the Boxer indemnity, however, one good thing has come. The Americans found that, after paying all just claims for damages, they still had a large surplus. This they returned to China to be spent on higher education, partly in colleges in China under American control, partly by sending advanced Chinese students to American universities. The gain to China has been enormous, and the benefit to America from the friendship of the Chinese (especially the most educated of them) is incalculable. This is obvious to everyone, yet England shows hardly any signs of following suit.

To understand the difficulties with which the Chinese Government is faced, it is necessary to realize the loss of fiscal independence which China has suffered as the result of the various wars and treaties which have been forced upon her. In the early days, the Chinese had no experience of European diplomacy, and did not know what to avoid; in later days, they have not been allowed to treat old treaties as scraps of paper, since that is the prerogative of the Great Powers—a prerogative which every single one of them exercises.

The best example of this state of affairs is the Customs tariff.[4] At the end of our first war with China, in 1842, we concluded a treaty which provided for a duty at treaty ports of 5 per cent on all imports and not more than 5 per cent on exports. This treaty is the basis of the whole Customs system. At the end of our next war, in 1858, we drew up a schedule of conventional prices on which the 5 per cent was to be calculated. This was to be revised every ten years, but has in fact only been revised twice, once in 1902 and once in 1918.[5] Revision of the schedule is merely a change in the conventional prices, not a change in the tariff, which remains fixed at 5 per cent. Change in the tariff is practically impossible, since China has concluded commercial treaties involving a most-favoured-nation clause, and the same tariff, with twelve States besides Great Britain, and therefore any change in the tariff requires the unanimous consent of thirteen Powers.

When foreign Powers speak of the Open Door as a panacea for China, it must be remembered that the Open Door does nothing to give the Chinese the usual autonomy as regards Customs that is enjoyed by other sovereign States.[6] The treaty of 1842, on which the system rests, has no time-limit or provision for denunciation by either party, such as other commercial treaties contain. A low tariff suits the Powers that wish to find a market for their goods in China, and they have therefore no motive for consenting to any alteration. In the past, when we practised free trade, we could defend ourselves by saying that the policy we forced upon China was the same as that which we adopted ourselves. But no other nation could make this excuse, nor can we now that we have abandoned free trade by the Safeguarding of Industries Act.

The import tariff being so low, the Chinese Government is compelled, for the sake of revenue, to charge the maximum of 5 per cent on all exports. This, of course, hinders the development of Chinese commerce, and is probably a mistake. But the need of sources of revenue is desperate, and it is not surprising that the Chinese authorities should consider the tax indispensable.

There is also another system in China, chiefly inherited from the time of the Taiping rebellion, namely the erection of internal customs barriers at various important points. This plan is still adopted with the internal trade. But merchants dealing with the interior and sending goods to or from a Treaty Port can escape internal customs by the payment of half the duty charged under the external tariff. As this is generally less than the internal tariff charges, this provision favours foreign produce at the expense of that of China. Of course the system of internal customs is bad, but it is traditional, and is defended on the ground that revenue is indispensable. China offered to abolish internal customs in return for certain uniform increases in the import and export tariff, and Great Britain, Japan, and the United States consented.

But there were ten other Powers whose consent was necessary, and not all could be induced to agree. So the old system remains in force, not chiefly through the fault of the Chinese central government. It should be added that internal customs are collected by the provincial authorities, who usually intercept them and use them for private armies and civil war. At the present time, the Central Government is not strong enough to stop these abuses.

The administration of the Customs is only partially in the hands of the Chinese. By treaty, the Inspector-General, who is at the head of the service, must be British so long as our trade with China exceeds that of any other treaty State; and the appointment of all subordinate officials is in his hands. In 1918 (the latest year for which I have the figures) there were 7,500 persons employed in the Customs, and of these 2,000 were non-Chinese. The first Inspector-General was Sir Robert Hart, who, by the unanimous testimony of all parties, fulfilled his duties exceedingly well. For the time being, there is much to be said for the present system. The Chinese have the appointment of the Inspector-General, and can therefore choose a man who is sympathetic to their country. Chinese officials are, as a rule, corrupt and indolent, so that control by foreigners is necessary in creating a modern bureaucracy. So long as the foreign officials are responsible to the Chinese Government, not to foreign States, they fulfil a useful educative function, and help to prepare the way for the creation of an efficient Chinese State. The problem for China is to secure practical and intellectual training from the white nations without becoming their slaves. In dealing with this problem, the system adopted in the Customs has much to recommend it during the early stages.[7]

At the same time, there are grave infringements of Chinese independence in the present position of the Customs, apart altogether from the fact that the tariff is fixed by treaty for ever. Much of the revenue derivable from customs is mortgaged for various loans and indemnities, so that the Customs cannot be dealt with from the point of view of Chinese interests alone. Moreover, in the present state of anarchy, the Customs administration can exercise considerable control over Chinese politics by recognizing or not recognizing a given *de facto* Government. (There is no Government *de jure*, at any rate in the North.) At present, the Customs Revenue is withheld in the South, and an artificial bankruptcy is being engineered. In view of the reactionary instincts of diplomats, this constitutes a terrible obstacle to internal reform. It means that no Government which is in earnest in attempting to introduce radical improvements can hope to enjoy the Customs revenue, which interposes a formidable fiscal barrier in the way of reconstruction.

There is a similar situation as regards the salt tax. This also was accepted as security for various foreign loans, and in order to make the security acceptable the foreign Powers concerned insisted upon the employment of foreigners in the principal posts. As in the case of the Customs, the foreign inspectors are appointed by the Chinese Government, and the situation is in all respects similar to that existing as regards the Customs.

The Customs and the salt tax form the security for various loans to China. This, together with foreign administration, gives opportunities of interference by the Powers which they show no inclination to neglect. The way in which the situation is utilized may be illustrated by three telegrams in *The Times* which appeared during January of this year.

On January 14, 1922, *The Times* published the following in a telegram from its Peking correspondent:

> It is curious to reflect that this country (China) could be rendered completely solvent and the Government provided with a substantial income almost by a stroke of the foreigner's pen, while without that stroke there must be bankruptcy, pure and simple. Despite constant civil war and political chaos, the Customs revenue consistently grows, and last year exceeded all records by £1,000,000. The increased duties sanctioned by the Washington Conference will provide sufficient revenue to liquidate the whole foreign and domestic floating debt in a very few years, leaving the splendid salt surplus unencumbered for the Government. The difficulty is not to provide money, but to find a Government to which to entrust it. Nor is there any visible prospect of the removal of this difficulty.

I venture to think *The Times* would regard the difficulty as removed if the Manchu Empire were restored.

As to the "splendid salt surplus," there are two telegrams from the Peking correspondent to *The Times* (of January 12th and 23rd, respectively) showing what we gain by making the Peking Government artificially bankrupt. The first telegram (sent on January 10th) is as follows:—

Present conditions in China are aptly illustrated by what is happening in one of the great salt revenue stations on the Yangtsze, near Chinkiang. That portion of the Chinese fleet faithful to the Central Government—the better half went over to the Canton Government long ago—has dispatched a squadron of gunboats to the salt station and notified Peking that if $3,000,000 (about £400,000) arrears of pay were not immediately forthcoming the amount would be forcibly recovered from the revenue. Meanwhile the immense salt traffic on the Yangtsze has been suspended. The Legations concerned have now sent an Identic Note to the Government warning it of the necessity for immediately securing the removal of the obstruction to the traffic and to the operations of the foreign collectorate.

The second telegram is equally interesting. It is as follows:—

The question of interference with the Salt Gabelle is assuming a serious aspect. The Chinese squadron of gunboats referred to in my message of the 10th is still blocking the salt traffic near Chingkiang, while a new intruder in the shape of an agent of Wu-Pei-Fu [the Liberal military leader] has installed himself in the collectorate at Hankow, and is endeavouring to appropriate the receipts for his powerful master. The British, French, and Japanese Ministers accordingly have again addressed the Government, giving notice that if these irregular proceedings do not cease they will be compelled to take independent action. The Reorganization Loan of £25,000,000 is secured on the salt revenues, and interference with the foreign control of the department constitutes an infringement of the loan agreement. In various parts of China, some independent of Peking, others not, the local *Tuchuns* (military governors) impound the collections and materially diminish the total coming under the control of the foreign inspectorate, but the balance remaining has been so large, and protest so useless, that hitherto all concerned have considered it expedient to acquiesce. But interference at points on the Yangtsze, where naval force can be brought to bear, is another matter. The situation is interesting in view of the amiable resolutions adopted at Washington, by which the Powers would seem to have debarred themselves, in the future, from any active form of intervention in this country. In view of the extensive opposition to the Liang Shih-yi Cabinet and the present interference with the salt negotiations, the $90,000,000 (£11,000,000) loan to be secured on the salt surplus has been dropped. The problem of how to weather the new year settlement on January 38th remains unsolved.

It is a pretty game: creating artificial bankruptcy, and then inflicting punishment for the resulting anarchy. How regrettable that the Washington Conference should attempt to interfere!

It is useless to deny that the Chinese have brought these troubles upon themselves, by their inability to produce capable and honest officials. This inability has its roots in Chinese ethics, which lay stress upon a man's duty to his family rather than to the public. An official is expected to keep all his relations supplied with funds, and therefore can only be honest at the expense of filial piety. The decay of the family system is a vital condition of progress in China. All Young China realizes this, and one may hope that twenty years hence the level of honesty among officials may be not lower in China than in Europe— no very extravagant hope. But for this purpose friendly contact with Western nations is essential. If we insist upon rousing Chinese nationalism as we have roused that of India and Japan, the Chinese will begin to think that wherever they differ from Europe, they differ for the better. There is more truth in this than Europeans like to think, but it is not wholly true, and if it comes to be believed our power for good in China will be at an end.

I have described briefly in this chapter what the Christian Powers did to China while they were able to act independently of Japan. But in modern China it is Japanese aggression that is the most urgent problem. Before considering this, however, we must deal briefly with the rise of modern Japan—a quite peculiar blend of East and West, which I hope is not prophetic of the blend to be ultimately achieved in China. But before passing to Japan, I will give a brief description of the social and political condition of modern China, without which Japan's action in China would be unintelligible.

## NOTES

1  In 1691 the Emperor Kang Hsi issued an edict explaining his attitude towards various religions. Of Roman Catholicism he says: "As to the western doctrine which glorifies *Tien Chu*, the Lord of the Sky, that, too, is heterodox; but because its priests are thoroughly conversant with mathematics, the Government makes use of them—a point which you soldiers and people should understand." (Giles, op. cit. p. 252.)

2  *Annals and Memoirs of the Court of Peking*, pp. 322 ff.

3  The Summer Palace now shown to tourists is modern, chiefly built by the Empress Dowager.

4  There is an admirable account of this question in Chap. vii. of Sih-Gung Cheng's *Modern China*, Clarendon Press, 1919.

5  A new revision has been decided upon by the Washington Conference.

6  If you lived in a town where the burglars had obtained possession of the Town Council, they would very likely insist upon the policy of the Open Door, but you might not consider it wholly satisfactory. Such is China's situation among the Great Powers.

7  *The Times* of November 26, 1921, had a leading article on Mr. Wellington Koo's suggestion, at Washington, that China ought to be allowed to recover fiscal autonomy as regards the tariff. Mr. Koo did not deal with the Customs *administration*, nevertheless *The Times* assumed that his purpose was to get the administration into the hands of the Chinese on account of the opportunities of lucrative corruption which it would afford. I wrote to *The Times* pointing out that they had confused the administration with the tariff, and that Mr. Koo was dealing only with the tariff. In view of the fact that they did not print either my letter or any other to the same effect, are we to conclude that their misrepresentation was deliberate and intentional?

# 4

# MODERN CHINA

THE position of China among the nations of the world is quite peculiar, because in population and potential strength China is the greatest nation in the world, while in actual strength at the moment it is one of the least. The international problems raised by this situation have been brought into the forefront of world-politics by the Washington Conference. What settlement, if any, will ultimately be arrived at, it is as yet impossible to foresee. There are, however, certain broad facts and principles which no wise solution can ignore, for which I shall try to give the evidence in the course of the following chapters, but which it may be as well to state briefly at the outset. First, the Chinese, though as yet incompetent in politics and backward in economic development, have, in other respects, a civilization at least as good as our own, containing elements which the world greatly needs, and which we shall destroy at our peril. Secondly, the Powers have inflicted upon China a multitude of humiliations and disabilities, for which excuses have been found in China's misdeeds, but for which the sole real reason has been China's military and naval weakness. Thirdly, the best of the Great Powers at present, in relation to China, is America, and the worst is Japan; in the interests of China, as well as in our own larger interests, it is an immense advance that we have ceased to support Japan and have ranged ourselves on the side of America, in so far as America stands for Chinese freedom, but not when Japanese freedom is threatened. Fourthly, in the long run, the Chinese cannot escape economic domination by foreign Powers unless China becomes military or the foreign Powers become Socialistic, because the capitalist system involves in its very essence a predatory relation of the strong towards the weak, internationally as well as nationally. A strong military China would be a disaster; therefore Socialism in Europe and America affords the only ultimate solution.

After these preliminary remarks, I come to the theme of this chapter, namely, the present internal condition of China.

As everyone knows, China, after having an Emperor for forty centuries, decided, eleven years ago, to become a modern democratic republic. Many causes led up to this result. Passing over the first 3,700 years of Chinese history, we arrive at the Manchu conquest in 1644, when a warlike invader from the north succeeded in establishing himself upon the Dragon Throne. He set to work to induce Chinese men to wear pigtails and Chinese women to have big feet. After a time a statesman-like compromise was arranged: pigtails were adopted but big feet were rejected; the new absurdity was accepted and the old one retained. This characteristic compromise shows how much England and China have in common.

The Manchu Emperors soon became almost completely Chinese, but differences of dress and manners kept the Manchus distinct from the more civilized people whom they had conquered, and the Chinese remained inwardly hostile to them. From 1840 to 1900, a series of disastrous foreign wars, culminating in the humiliation of the Boxer time, destroyed the prestige of the Imperial Family and showed all thoughtful people the need of learning from Europeans. The Taiping rebellion, which lasted for 15 years (1849–64), is thought by Putnam

Weale to have diminished the population by 150 millions,[1] and was almost as terrible a business as the Great War. For a long time it seemed doubtful whether the Manchus could suppress it, and when at last they succeeded (by the help of Gordon) their energy was exhausted. The defeat of China by Japan (1894–5) and the vengeance of the Powers after the Boxer rising (1900) finally opened the eyes of all thoughtful Chinese to the need for a better and more modern government than that of the Imperial Family. But things move slowly in China, and it was not till eleven years after the Boxer movement that the revolution broke out.

The revolution of 1911, in China, was a moderate one, similar in spirit to ours of 1688. Its chief promoter, Sun Yat Sen, now at the head of the Canton Government, was supported by the Republicans, and was elected provisional President. But the Northern Army remained faithful to the dynasty, and could probably have defeated the revolutionaries. Its Commander-in-Chief, Yuan Shih-k'ai, however, hit upon a better scheme. He made peace with the revolutionaries and acknowledged the Republic, on condition that he should be the first President instead of Sun Yat Sen. Yuan Shih-k'ai was, of course, supported by the Legations, being what is called a "strong man," i.e. a believer in blood and iron, not likely to be led astray by talk about democracy or freedom. In China, the North has always been more military and less liberal than the South, and Yuan Shih-k'ai had created out of Northern troops whatever China possessed in the way of a modern army. As he was also ambitious and treacherous, he had every quality needed for inspiring confidence in the diplomatic corps. In view of the chaos which has existed since his death, it must be admitted, however, that there was something to be said in favour of his policy and methods.

A Constituent Assembly, after enacting a provisional constitution, gave place to a duly elected Parliament, which met in April 1913 to determine the permanent constitution. Yuan soon began to quarrel with the Parliament as to the powers of the President, which the Parliament wished to restrict. The majority in Parliament was opposed to Yuan, but he had the preponderance in military strength. Under these circumstances, as was to be expected, constitutionalism was soon overthrown. Yuan made himself financially independent of Parliament (which had been duly endowed with the power of the purse) by unconstitutionally concluding a loan with the foreign banks. This led to a revolt of the South, which, however, Yuan quickly suppressed. After this, by various stages, he made himself virtually absolute ruler of China. He appointed his army lieutenants military governors of provinces, and sent Northern troops into the South. His regime might have lasted but for the fact that, in 1915, he tried to become Emperor, and was met by a successful revolt. He died in 1916—of a broken heart, it was said.

Since then there has been nothing but confusion in China. The military governors appointed by Yuan refused to submit to the Central Government when his strong hand was removed, and their troops terrorized the populations upon whom they were quartered. Ever since there has been civil war, not, as a rule, for any definite principle, but simply to determine which of various rival generals should govern various groups of provinces. There still remains the issue of North versus South, but this has lost most of its constitutional significance.

The military governors of provinces or groups of provinces, who are called Tuchuns, govern despotically in defiance of Peking, and commit depredations on the inhabitants of the districts over which they rule. They intercept the revenue, except the portions collected and administered by foreigners, such as the salt tax. They are nominally appointed by Peking, but in practice depend only upon the favour of the soldiers in their provinces. The Central Government is nearly bankrupt, and is usually unable to pay the soldiers, who live by loot and by such portions of the Tuchun's illgotten wealth as he finds it prudent to surrender to them. When any faction seemed near to complete victory, the Japanese supported its opponents, in order that civil discord might be prolonged. While I was in Peking, the three most important Tuchuns met there for a conference on the division of the spoils. They were barely civil to the President and the Prime Minister, who still officially represent China in the eyes of foreign Powers. The unfortunate nominal Government was obliged to pay to these three worthies, out of a bankrupt treasury, a sum which the newspapers stated to be nine million dollars, to secure their departure from the capital. The largest share went to Chang-tso-lin, the Viceroy of Manchuria and commonly said to be a tool of Japan. His share was paid to cover the expenses of an expedition to Mongolia, which had revolted; but no one for a moment supposed that he would undertake such an expedition, and in fact he has remained at Mukden ever since.[2]

In the extreme south, however, there has been established a Government of a different sort, for which it is possible to have some respect. Canton, which has always been the centre of Chinese radicalism, succeeded, in the autumn of 1920, in throwing off the tyranny of its Northern garrison and establishing a progressive efficient Government under the Presidency of Sun Yat Sen. This Government now embraces two provinces, Kwangtung (of which Canton is the capital) and Kwangsi. For a moment it seemed likely to conquer the whole of the South, but it has been checked by the victories of the Northern General Wu-Pei-Fu in the neighbouring province of Hunan. Its enemies allege that it cherishes designs of conquest, and wishes to unite all China under its sway.[3] In all ascertainable respects it is a Government which deserves the support of all progressive people. Professor Dewey, in articles in the *New Republic,* has set forth its merits, as well as the bitter enmity which it has encountered from Hong-Kong and the British generally. This opposition is partly on general principles, because we dislike radical reform, partly because of the Cassel agreement. This agreement—of a common type in China—would have given us a virtual monopoly of the railways and mines in the province of Kwangtung. It had been concluded with the former Government, and only awaited ratification, but the change of Government has made ratification impossible. The new Government, very properly, is befriended by the Americans, and one of them, Mr. Shank, concluded an agreement with the new Government more or less similar to that which we had concluded with the old one. The American Government, however, did not support Mr. Shank, whereas the British Government did support the Cassel agreement. Meanwhile we have lost a very valuable though very iniquitous concession, merely because we, but not the Americans, prefer what is old and corrupt to what is vigorous and honest. I understand, moreover, that the Shank agreement lapsed because Mr. Shank could not raise the necessary capital.

The anarchy in China is, of course, very regrettable, and every friend of China must hope that it will be brought to an end. But it would be a mistake to exaggerate the evil, or to suppose that it is comparable in magnitude to the evils endured in Europe. China must not be compared to a single European country, but to Europe as a whole. In *The Times* of November 11, 1921, I notice a pessimistic article headed: "The Peril of China. A dozen rival Governments." But in Europe there are much more than a dozen Governments, and their enmities are much fiercer than those of China. The number of troops in Europe is enormously greater than in China, and they are infinitely better provided with weapons of destruction. The amount of fighting in Europe since the Armistice has been incomparably more than the amount in China during the same period. You may travel through China from end to end, and it is ten to one that you will see no signs of war. Chinese battles are seldom bloody, being fought by mercenary soldiers who take no interest in the cause for which they are supposed to be fighting. I am inclined to think that the inhabitants of China, at the present moment, are happier, on the average, than the inhabitants of Europe taken as a whole.

It is clear, I think, that political reform in China, when it becomes possible, will have to take the form of a federal constitution, allowing a very large measure of autonomy to the provinces. The division into provinces is very ancient, and provincial feeling is strong. After the revolution, a constitution more or less resembling our own was attempted, only with a President instead of a King. But the successful working of a non-federal constitution requires a homogeneous population without much local feeling, as may be seen from our own experience in Ireland. Most progressive Chinese, as far as I was able to judge, now favour a federal constitution, leaving to the Central Government not much except armaments, foreign affairs, and customs. But the difficulty of getting rid of the existing military anarchy is very great. The Central Government cannot disband the troops, because it cannot find the money to pay them. It would be necessary to borrow from abroad enough money to pay off the troops and establish them in new jobs. But it is doubtful whether any Power or Powers would make such a loan without exacting the sacrifice of the last remnants of Chinese independence. One must therefore hope that somehow the Chinese will find a way of escaping from their troubles without too much foreign assistance.

It is by no means impossible that one of the Tuchuns may become supreme, and may then make friends with the constitutionalists as the best way of consolidating his influence. China is a country where public opinion has great weight, and where the desire to be thought well of may quite possibly lead a successful militarist into patriotic courses. There are, at the moment, two Tuchuns who are more important than any of the others. These are Chang-tso-lin and Wu-Pei-Fu, both of whom have been already mentioned. Chang-tso-lin is supreme in Manchuria, and strong in Japanese support; he represents all that is most reactionary in China. Wu-Pei-Fu, on the other hand, is credited with liberal tendencies. He is an able general; not long ago, nominally at the bidding of Peking, he established his authority on the Yangtze and in Hunan, thereby dealing a blow to the hopes of Canton. It is not easy to see how he could come to terms with the Canton Government, especially since it has allied itself with Chang-tso-lin, but in the rest of China he might establish his authority and seek to make it permanent by being constitutional (see Appendix). If so, China might have a breathing-space, and a breathing-space is all that is needed.

The economic life of China, except in the Treaty Ports and in a few regions where there are mines, is still wholly pre-industrial. Peking has nearly a million inhabitants, and covers an enormous area, owing to the fact that all the houses have only a ground floor and are built round a courtyard. Yet it has no trams or buses or local trains. So far as I could see, there are not more than two or three factory chimneys in the whole town. Apart from begging, trading, thieving and Government employment, people live by handicrafts. The products are exquisite and the work less monotonous than machine-minding, but the hours are long and the pay infinitesimal.

Seventy or eighty per cent of the population of China are engaged in agriculture. Rice and tea are the chief products of the south, while wheat and other kinds of grain form the staple crops in the north.[4] The rainfall is very great in the south, but in the north it is only just sufficient to prevent the land from being a desert. When I arrived in China, in the autumn of 1920, a large area in the north, owing to drought, was afflicted with a terrible famine, nearly as bad, probably, as the famine in Russia in 1921. As the Bolsheviks were not concerned, foreigners had no hesitation in trying to bring relief. As for the Chinese, they regarded it passively as a stroke of fate, and even those who died of it shared this view.

Most of the land is in the hands of peasant proprietors, who divide their holdings among their sons, so that each man's share becomes barely sufficient to support himself and his family. Consequently, when the rainfall is less than usual, immense numbers perish of starvation. It would of course be possible, for a time, to prevent famines by more scientific methods of agriculture, and to prevent droughts and floods by afforestation. More railways and better roads would give a vastly improved market, and might greatly enrich the peasants for a generation. But in the long run, if the birth-rate is as great as is usually supposed, no permanent cure for their poverty is possible while their families continue to be so large. In China, Malthus's theory of population, according to many writers, finds full scope.[5] If so, the good done by any improvement of methods will lead to the survival of more children, involving a greater subdivision of the land, and in the end, a return to the same degree of poverty. Only education and a higher standard of life can remove the fundamental cause of these evils. And popular education, on a large scale, is of course impossible until there is a better Government and an adequate revenue. Apart even from these difficulties, there does not exist, as yet, a sufficient supply of competent Chinese teachers for a system of universal elementary education.

Apart from war, the impact of European civilization upon the traditional life of China takes two forms, one commercial, the other intellectual. Both depend upon the prestige of armaments; the Chinese

would never have opened either their ports to our trade or their minds
to our ideas if we had not defeated them in war. But the military
beginning of our intercourse with the Middle Kingdom has now re-
ceded into the background; one is not conscious, in any class, of a
strong hostility to foreigners as such. It would not be difficult to make
out a case for the view that intercourse with the white races is proving
a misfortune to China, but apparently this view is not taken by anyone
in China except where unreasoning conservative prejudice outweighs
all other considerations. The Chinese have a very strong instinct for
trade, and a considerable intellectual curiosity, to both of which we
appeal. Only a bare minimum of common decency is required to secure their friendship, whether privately or politically. And I think their
thought is as capable of enriching our culture as their commerce of
enriching our pockets.

In the Treaty Ports, Europeans and Americans live in their own
quarters, with streets well paved and lighted, houses in European style,
and shops full of American and English goods. There is generally also
a Chinese part of the town, with narrow streets, gaily decorated shops,
and the rich mixture of smells characteristic of China. Often one passes
through a gate, suddenly, from one to the other; after the cheerful dis-
ordered beauty of the old town, Europe's ugly cleanliness and Sunday-
go-to-meeting decency make a strange complex impression, half-love
and half-hate. In the European town one finds safety, spaciousness and
hygiene; in the Chinese town, romance, overcrowding and disease.
In spite of my affection for China, these transitions always made me
realize that I am a European; for me, the Chinese manner of life would
not mean happiness. But after making all necessary deductions for the
poverty and the disease, I am inclined to think that Chinese life brings
more happiness to the Chinese than English life does to us. At any rate
this seemed to me to be true for the men; for the women I do not
think it would be true.

Shanghai and Tientsin are white men's cities; the first sight of
Shanghai makes one wonder what is the use of travelling, because
there is so little change from what one is used to. Treaty Ports, each

of which is a centre of European influence, exist practically all over China, not only on the sea coast. Hankow, a very important Treaty Port, is almost exactly in the centre of China. North and South China are divided by the Yangtze; East and West China are divided by the route from Peking to Canton. These two dividing lines meet at Hankow, which has long been an important strategical point in Chinese history. From Peking to Hankow there is a railway, formerly Franco-Belgian, now owned by the Chinese Government. From Wuchang, opposite Hankow on the southern bank of the river, there is to be a railway to Canton, but at present it only runs half-way, to Changsha, also a Treaty Port. The completion of the railway, together with improved docks, will greatly increase the importance of Canton and diminish that of Hong-Kong.

In the Treaty Ports commerce is the principal business; but in the lower Yangtze and in certain mining districts there are beginnings of industrialism. China produces large amounts of raw cotton, which are mostly manipulated by primitive methods; but there are a certain number of cotton-mills on modern lines. If low wages meant cheap labour for the employer, there would be little hope for Lancashire, because in Southern China the cotton is grown on the spot, the climate is damp, and there is an inexhaustible supply of industrious coolies ready to work very long hours for wages upon which an English working-man would find it literally impossible to keep body and soul together. Nevertheless, it is not the underpaid Chinese coolie whom Lancashire has to fear, and China will not become a formidable competitor until improvement in methods and education enables the Chinese workers to earn good wages. Meanwhile, in China, as in every other country, the beginnings of industry are sordid and cruel. The intellectuals wish to be told of some less horrible method by which their country may be industrialized, but so far none is in sight.

The intelligentsia in China has a very peculiar position, unlike that which it has in any other country. Hereditary aristocracy has been practically extinct in China for about 2,000 years, and for many centuries the country has been governed by the successful candidates in competitive examinations. This has given to the educated the kind of prestige elsewhere belonging to a governing aristocracy. Although the old traditional education is fast dying out, and higher education now teaches modern subjects, the prestige of education has survived, and public opinion is still ready to be influenced by those who have intellectual qualifications. The Tuchuns, many of whom, including Chang-tso-lin, have begun by being brigands,[6] are, of course, mostly too stupid and ignorant to share this attitude, but that in itself makes their régime weak and unstable. The influence of Young China—i.e. of those who have been educated either abroad or in modern colleges at home—is far greater than it would be in a country with less respect for learning. This is, perhaps, the most hopeful feature in the situation, because the number of modern students is rapidly increasing, and their outlook and aims are admirable. In another ten years or so they will probably be strong enough to regenerate China—if only the Powers will allow ten years to elapse without taking any drastic action.

It is important to try to understand the outlook and potentialities of Young China. Most of my time was spent among those Chinese who had had a modern education, and I should like to give some idea of their mentality. It seemed to me that one could already distinguish two generations: the older men, who had fought their way with great difficulty and almost in solitude out of the traditional Confucian prejudices; and the younger men, who had found modern schools and colleges waiting for them, containing a whole world of modern-minded people ready to give sympathy and encouragement in the inevitable fight against the family. The older men—men varying in age from 30 to 50—have gone through an inward and outward struggle resembling that of the rationalists of Darwin's and Mill's generation. They have had, painfully and with infinite difficulty, to free their minds from the beliefs instilled in youth, and to turn their thoughts to a new science and a new ethic. Imagine (say) Plotinus recalled from the shades and miraculously compelled to respect Mr. Henry Ford; this will give you some idea of the centuries across which these men have had to travel in becoming European. Some of them are a little weary with the effort, their forces somewhat spent and their originality no longer creative. But this can astonish no one who realizes the internal revolution they have achieved in their own minds.

It must not be supposed that an able Chinaman, when he masters our culture, becomes purely imitative. This may happen among the second-rate Chinese, especially when they turn Christians, but it does not happen among the best. They remain Chinese, critical of European civilization even when they have assimilated it. They retain a certain crystal candour and a touching belief in the efficacy of moral forces; the industrial revolution has not yet affected their mental processes. When they become persuaded of the importance of some opinion, they try to spread it by setting forth the reasons in its favour; they do not hire the front pages of newspapers for advertising, or put up on hoardings along the railways "So-and-so's opinion is the best." In all this they differ greatly from more advanced nations, and particularly from America; it never occurs to them to treat opinions as if they were soaps. And they have no admiration for ruthlessness, or love of bustling activity without regard to its purpose. Having thrown over the prejudices in which they were brought up, they have not taken on a new set, but have remained genuinely free in their thoughts, able to consider any proposition honestly on its merits.

The younger men, however, have something more than the first generation of modern intellectuals. Having had less of a struggle, they have retained more energy and self-confidence. The candour and honesty of the pioneers survive, with more determination to be socially effective. This may be merely the natural character of youth, but I think it is more than that. Young men under thirty have often come in contact with Western ideas at a sufficiently early age to have assimilated them without a great struggle, so that they can acquire knowledge without being torn by spiritual conflicts. And they have been able to learn Western knowledge from Chinese teachers to begin with, which has made the process less difficult. Even the youngest students, of course, still have reactionary families, but they find less difficulty than their predecessors in resisting the claims of the family, and in realizing practically, not only theoretically, that the traditional Chinese reverence for the old may well be carried too far. In these young men I see the hope of China. When a little experience has taught them practical wisdom, I believe they will be able to lead Chinese opinion in the directions in which it ought to move.

There is one traditional Chinese belief which dies very hard, and that is the belief that correct ethical sentiments are more important than detailed scientific knowledge. This view is, of course, derived from the Confucian tradition, and is more or less true in a pre-industrial society. It would have been upheld by Rousseau or Dr. Johnson, and broadly speaking by everybody before the Bentha-mites. We, in the West, have now swung to the opposite extreme: we tend to think that technical efficiency is everything and moral purpose nothing. A battleship may be taken as the concrete embodiment of this view. When we read, say, of some new poison-gas by means of which one bomb from an aeroplane can exterminate a whole town, we have a thrill of what we fondly believe to be horror, but it is really delight in scientific skill. Science is our god; we say to it, "Though thou slay me, yet will I trust in thee." And so it slays us. The Chinese have not this defect, but they have the opposite one, of believing that good intentions are the only thing really necessary. I will give an illustration. Forsythe Sherfesee, Forestry Adviser to the Chinese Government, gave an address at the British Legation in January 1919 on "Some National Aspects of Forestry in China."[7] In this address he proves (so far as a person ignorant of forestry can judge) that large parts of China which now lie waste are suitable for forestry, that the importation of timber (*e.g.* for railway sleepers) which now takes place is wholly unnecessary, and that the floods which often sweep away whole districts would be largely prevented if the slopes of the mountains from which the rivers come were re-afforested. Yet it is often difficult to interest even the most reforming Chinese in afforestation, because it is not an easy subject for ethical enthusiasm. Trees are planted round graves, because Confucius said they should be; if Confucianism dies out, even these will be cut down. But public-spirited Chinese students learn political theory as it is taught in our universities, and despise such humble questions as the utility of trees. After learning all about (say) the proper relations of the two Houses of Parliament, they go home to find that some Tuchun has dismissed both Houses, and is governing in a fashion not considered in our text-books. Our theories of politics are only true in the West (if there); our theories of forestry are equally true everywhere. Yet it is our theories of politics that Chinese students are most eager to learn. Similarly the practical study of industrial processes might be very useful, but the Chinese prefer the study of our theoretical economics, which is hardly applicable except where industry is already developed. In all these respects, however, there is beginning to be a marked improvement.

It is science that makes the difference between our intellectual outlook and that of the Chinese intelligentsia. The Chinese, even the most modern, look to the white nations, especially America, for moral maxims to replace those of Confucius. They have not yet grasped that men's morals in the mass are the same everywhere: they do as much harm as they dare, and as much good as they must. In so far as there is a difference of morals between us and the Chinese, we differ for the worse, because we are more energetic, and can therefore commit more crimes per diem. What we have to teach the Chinese is not morals, or ethical maxims about government, but science and technical skill. The real problem for the Chinese intellectuals is to acquire Western knowledge without acquiring the mechanistic outlook.

Perhaps it is not clear what I mean by "the mechanistic outlook." I mean something which exists equally in Imperialism, Bolshevism and the Y.M.C.A.; something which distinguishes all these from the Chinese outlook, and which I, for my part, consider very evil. What I mean is the habit of regarding mankind as raw material, to be moulded by our scientific manipulation into whatever form may happen to suit our fancy. The essence of the matter, from the point of view of the individual who has this point of view, is the cultivation of will at the expense of perception, the fervent moral belief that it is our duty to force other people to realize our conception of the world. The Chinese intellectual is not much troubled by Imperialism as a creed, but is vigorously assailed by Bolshevism and the Y.M.C.A., to one or other of which he is too apt to fall a victim, learning a belief from the one in the class-war and the dictatorship of the communists, from the other in the mystic efficacy of cold baths and dumb-bells. Both these creeds, in their Western adepts, involve a contempt for the rest of mankind except as potential converts, and the belief that progress consists in the spread of a doctrine. They both involve a belief in government and a life against Nature. This view, though I have called it mechanistic, is as old as religion, though mechanism has given it new and more virulent forms. The first of Chinese philosophers, Lao-Tze, wrote his book to protest against it, and his disciple Chuang-Tze put his criticism into a fable[8]:—

> Horses have hoofs to carry them over frost and snow; hair, to protect them from wind and cold. They eat grass and drink water, and fling up their heels over the champaign. Such is the real nature of horses. Palatial dwellings are of no use to them.
>
> One day Po Lo appeared, saying: "I understand the management of horses."
>
> So he branded them, and clipped them, and pared their hoofs, and put halters on them, tying them up by the head and shackling them by the feet, and disposing them in stables, with the result that two or three in every ten died. Then he kept them hungry and thirsty, trotting them and galloping them, and grooming, and trimming, with the misery of the tasselled bridle before and the fear of the knotted whip behind, until more than half of them were dead.
>
> The potter says: "I can do what I will with clay. If I want it round, I use compasses; if rectangular, a square."
>
> The carpenter says: "I can do what I will with wood. If I want it curved, I use an arc; if straight, a line."
>
> But on what grounds can we think that the natures of clay and wood desire this application of compasses and square, of arc and

line? Nevertheless, every age extols Po Lo for his skill in managing horses, and potters and carpenters for their skill with clay and wood. Those who *govern* the Empire make the same mistake.

Although Taoism, of which Lao-Tze was the founder and Chuang-Tze the chief apostle, was displaced by Confucianism, yet the spirit of this fable has penetrated deeply into Chinese life, making it more urbane and tolerant, more contemplative and observant, than the fiercer life of the West. The Chinese watch foreigners as we watch animals in the Zoo, to see whether they "drink water and fling up their heels over the champaign," and generally to derive amusement from their curious habits. Unlike the Y.M.C.A., they have no wish to alter the habits of the foreigners, any more than we wish to put the monkeys at the Zoo into trousers and stiff shirts. And their attitude towards each other is, as a rule, equally tolerant. When they became a Republic, instead of cutting off the Emperor's head, as other nations do, they left him his title, his palace, and four million dollars a year (about £600,000), and he remains to this moment with his officials, his eunuchs and his etiquette, but without one shred of power or influence. In talking with a Chinese, you feel that he is trying to understand you, not to alter you or interfere with you. The result of his attempt may be a caricature or a panegyric, but in either case it will be full of delicate perception and subtle humour. A friend in Peking showed me a number of pictures, among which I specially remember various birds: a hawk swooping on a sparrow, an eagle clasping a big bough of a tree in his claws, water-fowl standing on one leg disconsolate in the snow. All these pictures showed that kind of sympathetic understanding which one feels also in their dealings with human beings—something which I can perhaps best describe as the antithesis of Nietzsche. This quality, unfortunately, is useless in warfare, and foreign nations are doing their best to stamp it out. But it is an infinitely valuable quality, of which our Western world has far too little. Together with their exquisite sense of beauty, it makes the Chinese nation quite extraordinarily lovable. The injury that we are doing to China is wanton and cruel, the destruction of something delicate and lovely for the sake of the gross pleasures of barbarous millionaires. One of the poems translated from the Chinese by Mr. Waley[9] is called *Business Men*, and it expresses, perhaps more accurately than I could do, the respects in which the Chinese are our superiors:—

> Business men boast of their skill and cunning
> But in philosophy they are like little children.
> Bragging to each other of successful depredations
> They neglect to consider the ultimate fate of the body.
> What should they know of the Master of Dark Truth
> Who saw the wide world in a jade cup,
> By illumined conception got clear of heaven and earth:
> On the chariot of Mutation entered the Gate of Immutability?

I wish I could hope that some respect for "the Master of Dark Truth" would enter into the hearts of our apostles of Western culture. But as that is out of the question, it is necessary to seek other ways of solving the Far Eastern question.

## NOTES

1   *The Truth about China and Japan*, Allen & Unwin, 1921, p. 14. On the other hand Sih-Gung Cheng (*Modern China*, p. 13) says that it "killed twenty million people" which is the more usual estimate, cf. *China of the Chinese* by E. T. C. Werner, p. 24. The extent to which the population was diminished is not accurately known, but I have no doubt that 20 millions is nearer the truth than 150 millions.

2   In January 1922, he came to Peking to establish a more subservient Government, the dismissal of which has been ordered by Wu-Pei-Fu. A clash is imminent. See Appendix.

3   The blame for this is put upon Sun Yat Sen, who is said to have made an alliance with Chang-tso-lin. The best element in the Canton Government was said to be represented by Sun's colleague General Cheng Chiung Ming, who is now reported to have been dismissed (*The Times*, April 24, 1922). These statements are apparently unfounded. See Appendix.

4   The soya bean is rapidly becoming an important product, especially in Manchuria.

5   There are, however, no accurate statistics as to the birth-rate or the death-rate in China, and some writers question whether the birth-rate is really very large. From a privately printed pamphlet by my friend Mr. V. K. Ting, I learn that Dr. Lennox, of the Peking Union Medical College, from a careful study of 4,000 families, found that the average number of children (dead and living) per family was 21, while the infant mortality was 184.1. Other investigations are quoted to show that the birth-rate near Peking is between 30 and 50. In the absence of statistics, generalizations about the population question in China must be received with extreme caution.

6   I repeat what everybody, Chinese or foreign, told me. Mr. Bland, *per contra*, describes Chang-tso-lin as a polished Confucian. Contrast p. 104 of his *China, Japan and Korea* with pp. 143, 146 of Coleman's *The Far East Unveiled*, which gives the view of everybody except Mr. Bland. Lord Northcliffe had an interview with Chang-tso-lin reported in *The Times* recently, but he was, of course, unable to estimate Chang-tso-lin's claims to literary culture.

7   Printed in *China in* 1918, published by the *Peking Leader*.

8   *Musings of a Chinese Mystic*, by Lionel Giles (Murray), p. 66. For Legge's translation, see Vol. I, p. 277 of his *Texts of Taoism* in *Sacred Books of the East*, Vol. XXXIX.

9   Waley, 170 *Chinese Poems*, p. 95.

# 5

# JAPAN BEFORE THE
# RESTORATION

For modern China, the most important foreign nation is Japan. In order to understand the part played by Japan, it is necessary to know something of that country, to which we must now turn our attention.

In reading the history of Japan, one of the most amazing things is the persistence of the same forces and the same beliefs throughout the centuries. Japanese history practically begins with a "Restoration" by no means unlike that of 1867–8. Buddhism was introduced into Japan from Korea in 552 A.D.[1] At the same time and from the same source Chinese civilization became much better known in Japan than it had been through the occasional intercourse of former centuries. Both novelties won favour. Two Japanese students (followed later by many others) went to China in 608 A.D., to master the civilization of that country. The Japanese are an experimental nation, and before adopting Buddhism nationally they ordered one or two prominent courtiers to adopt it, with a view to seeing whether they prospered more or less than the adherents of the traditional Shinto religion.[2] After some vicissitudes, the experiment was held to have favoured the foreign religion, which, as a Court religion, acquired more prestige than Shinto, although the latter was never ousted, and remained the chief religion of the peasantry until the thirteenth century. It is remarkable to find that, as late as the sixteenth century, Hideyoshi, who was of peasant origin, had a much higher opinion of "the way of the gods" (which is what "Shinto" means) than of Buddhism.[3] Probably the revival of Shinto in modern times was facilitated by a continuing belief in that religion on the part of the less noisy sections of the population. But so far as the people mentioned in history are concerned, Buddhism plays a very much greater part than Shinto.

The object of the Restoration in 1867–8 was, at any rate in part, to restore the constitution of 645 A.D. The object of the constitution of 645 A.D. was to restore the form of government that had prevailed in the good old days. What the object was of those who established the government of the good old days, I do not profess to know. However that may be, the country before 645 A.D. was given over to feudalism and internal strife, while the power of the Mikado had sunk to a very low ebb. The Mikado had had the civil power, but had allowed great feudatories to acquire military control, so that the civil government fell into contempt. Contact with the superior civilization of China made intelligent people think that the Chinese constitution deserved imitation, along with the Chinese morals and religion.

The Chinese Emperor was the Son of Heaven, so the Mikado came to be descended from the Sun Goddess. The Chinese Emperor, whenever he happened to be a vigorous man, was genuinely supreme, so the Mikado must be made so.

The similarity of the influence of China in producing the Restoration of 645 A.D. and that of Europe in producing the Restoration of 1867–8 is set forth by Murdoch[4] as follows:—

In the summer of 1863 a band of four Choshu youths were smuggled on board a British steamer by the aid of kind Scottish friends who sympathized with their endeavour to proceed to Europe for purposes of study. These friends possibly did not know that some of the four had been protagonists in the burning down of the British Legation on Goten-yama a few months before, and they certainly could never have suspected that the real mission of the four youths was to master the secrets of Western civilization with a sole view of driving the Western barbarians from the sacred soil of Japan. Prince Ito and Marquis Inouye—for they were two of this venturesome quartette—have often told of their rapid disillusionment when they reached London, and saw these despised Western barbarians at home. On their return to Japan they at once became the apostles of a new doctrine, and their effective preaching has had much to do with the pride of place Dai Nippon now holds among the Great Powers of the world.

The two students who went to China in 608 A.D. "rendered even more illustrious service to their country perhaps than Ito and Inouye have done. For at the Revolution of 1868, the leaders of the movement harked back to the 645–650 A.D. period for a good deal of their inspiration, and the real men of political knowledge at that time were the two National Doctors."

Politically, what was done in 645 A.D. and the period immediately following was not unlike what was done in France by Louis XI and Richelieu—a curbing of the great nobles and an exaltation of the sovereign, with a substitution of civil justice for military anarchy. The movement was represented by its promoters as a Restoration, probably with about the same amount of truth as in 1867. At the latter date, there was restoration so far as the power of the Mikado was concerned, but innovation as regards the introduction of Western ideas. Similarly, in 645 A.D., what was done about the Mikado was a return to the past, but what was done in the way of spreading Chinese civilization was just the opposite. There must have been, in both cases, the same curious mixture of antiquarian and reforming tendencies.

Throughout subsequent Japanese history, until the Restoration, one seems to see two opposite forces struggling for mastery over people's minds, namely the ideas of government, civilization and art derived from China on the one hand, and the native tendency to feudalism, clan government, and civil war on the other. The conflict is very analogous to that which went on in mediaeval Europe between the Church, which represented ideas derived from Rome, and the turbulent barons, who were struggling to preserve the way of life of the ancient Teutons. Henry IV at Canossa, Henry II doing penance for Becket, represent the triumph of civilization over rude vigour; and something similar is to be seen at intervals in Japan.

After 645, the Mikado's Government had real power for some centuries, but gradually it fell more and more under the sway of the soldiers. So long as it had wealth (which lasted long after it ceased to have power) it continued to represent what was most civilized in Japan: the study of Chinese literature, the patronage of art, and the attempt to preserve respect for something other than brute force. But the Court nobles (who remained throughout quite distinct from the military feudal chiefs) were so degenerate and feeble, so stereotyped and unprogressive, that it would have been quite impossible for the country to be governed by them and the system they represented. In this respect they differed greatly from the mediaeval Church, which no one could accuse of lack of vigour, although the vigour of the feudal aristocracy may have been even greater. Accordingly, while the Church in Europe usually defeated the secular princes, the exact opposite happened in Japan, where the Mikado and his Court sank into greater and greater contempt down to the time of the Restoration.

The Japanese have a curious passion for separating the real and the nominal Governments, leaving the show to the latter and the substance of power to the former. First the Emperors took to resigning in favour of their infant sons, and continuing to govern in reality, often from some monastery, where they had become monks. Then the Shogun, who represented the military power, became supreme, but still governed in the name of the Emperor. The word "Shogun" merely means "General"; the full title of the people whom we call "Shogun" is "Sei-i-Tai Shogun," which means "Barbarian-subduing great General"; the barbarians in question being the Ainus, the Japanese aborigines. The first to hold this office in the form which it had at most times until the Restoration was Minamoto Yoritomo, on whom the title was conferred by the Mikado in 1192. But before long the Shogun became nearly as much of a figure-head as the Mikado. Custom confined the Shogunate to the Minamoto family, and the actual power was wielded by Regents in the name of the Shogun. This lasted until near the end of the sixteenth century, when it happened that Iyeyasu, the supreme military commander of his day, belonged to the Minamoto family, and was therefore able to assume the office of Shogun himself. He and his descendants held the office until it was abolished at the Restoration. The Restoration, however, did not put an end to the practice of a real Government behind the nominal one. The Prime Minister and his Cabinet are presented to the world as the Japanese Government, but the real Government is the Genro, or Elder Statesmen, and their successors, of whom I shall have more to say in the next chapter.

What the Japanese made of Buddhism reminds one in many ways of what the Teutonic nations made of Christianity. Buddhism and Christianity, originally, were very similar in spirit. They were both religions aiming at the achievement of holiness by renunciation of the world. They both ignored politics and government and wealth, for which they substituted the future life as what was of real importance. They were both religions of peace, teaching gentleness and non-resistance. But both had to undergo great transformations in adapting themselves to the instincts of warlike barbarians. In Japan, a multitude of sects arose, teaching doctrines which differed in many ways from Mahayana orthodoxy. Buddhism became national and militaristic; the abbots of great monasteries became important feudal chieftains, whose monks constituted an army which was ready to fight on the slightest provocation. Sieges of monasteries and battles with monks are of constant occurrence in Japanese history.

The Japanese, as every one knows, decided, after about 100 years' experience of Western missionaries and merchants, to close their country completely to foreigners, with the exception of a very restricted and closely supervised commerce with the Dutch. The first arrival of the Portuguese in Japan was in or about the year 1543, and their final expulsion was in the year 1639. What happened between these two dates is instructive for the understanding of Japan. The first

Portuguese brought with them Christianity and fire-arms, of which
the Japanese tolerated the former for the sake of the latter. At that time
there was virtually no Central Government in the country, and the
various Daimyo were engaged in constant wars with each other. The
south-western island, Kyushu, was even more independent of such
central authority as existed than were the other parts of Japan, and
it was in this island (containing the port of Nagasaki) that the Portuguese first landed and were throughout chiefly active. They traded
from Macao, bringing merchandise, matchlocks and Jesuits, as well as
artillery on their larger vessels. It was found that they attached importance to the spread of Christianity, and some of the Daimyo, in order
to get their trade and their guns, allowed themselves to be baptized by
the Jesuits. The Portuguese of those days seem to have been genuinely
more anxious to make converts than to extend their trade; when, later
on, the Japanese began to object to missionaries while still desiring
trade, neither the Portuguese nor the Spaniards could be induced to
refrain from helping the Fathers. However, all might have gone well if
the Portuguese had been able to retain the monopoly which had been
granted to them by a Papal Bull. Their monopoly of trade was associated with a Jesuit monopoly of missionary activity. But from 1592 on-
ward, the Spaniards from Manila competed with the Portuguese from
Macao, and the Dominican and Franciscan missionaries, brought by
the Spaniards, competed with the Jesuit missionaries brought by the
Portuguese. They quarrelled furiously, even at times when they were
suffering persecution; and the Japanese naturally believed the accusa-
tions that each side brought against the other. Moreover, when they
were shown maps displaying the extent of the King of Spain's dominions, they became alarmed for their national independence. In the year
1596, a Spanish ship, the *San Felipe*, on its way from Manila to Acapulco,
was becalmed off the coast of Japan. The local Daimyo insisted on
sending men to tow it into his harbour, and gave them instructions to
run it aground on a sandbank, which they did. He thereupon claimed
the whole cargo, valued at 600,000 crowns. However, Hideyoshi, who
was rapidly acquiring supreme power in Japan, thought this too large
a windfall for a private citizen, and had the Spanish pilot interviewed

by a man named Masuda. The pilot, after trying reason in vain, attempted intimidation.

> He produced a map of the world, and on it pointed out the vast extent of the dominions of Philip II. Thereupon Masuda asked him how it was so many countries had been brought to acknowledge the sway of a single man. . . ."Our Kings," said this outspoken seaman, "begin by sending into the countries they wish to conquer *religieux* who induce the people to embrace our religion, and when they have made considerable progress, troops are sent who combine with the new Christians, and then our Kings have not much trouble in accomplishing the rest."[5]

As Spain and Portugal were at this time both subject to Philip II, the Portuguese also suffered from the suspicions engendered by this speech. Moreover, the Dutch, who were at war with Spain, began to trade with Japan, and to tell all they knew against Jesuits, Dominicans, Franciscans, and Papists generally. A breezy Elizabethan sea captain, Will Adams, was wrecked in Japan, and on being interrogated naturally gave a good British account of the authors of the Armada. As the Japanese had by this time mastered the use and manufacture of firearms, they began to think that they had nothing more to learn from Christian nations.

Meanwhile, a succession of three great men—Nobunaga, Hideyoshi, and Iyeyasu—had succeeded in unifying Japan, destroying the quasi-independence of the feudal nobles, and establishing that reign of internal peace which lasted until the Restoration— a period of nearly two and a half centuries. It was possible, therefore, for the Central Government to enforce whatever policy it chose to adopt with regard to the foreigners and their religion. The Jesuits and the Friars between them had made a considerable number of converts in Japan, probably about 300,000. Most of these were in the island of Kyushu, the last region to be subdued by Hideyoshi. They tended to disloyalty, not only on account of their Christianity, but also on account of their geographical position. It was in this region that the revolt against the Shogun began in 1867, and Satsuma, the chief clan in the island of Kyushu, has had great power in the Government ever since the Restoration, except during its rebellion of 1877. It is hard to disentangle what belongs to Christianity and what to mere hostility to the Central Government in the movements of the sixteenth and seventeenth centuries. However that may be, Iyeyasu decided to persecute the Christians vigorously, if possible without losing the foreign trade. His successors were even more anti-Christian and less anxious for trade. After an abortive revolt in 1637, Christianity was stamped out, and foreign trade was prohibited in the most vigorous terms:—

> So long as the sun warms the earth, let no Christian be so bold as to come to Japan, and let all know that if King Philip himself, or even the very God of the Christians, or the great Shaka contravene this prohibition, they shall pay for it with their heads.[6]

The persecution of the Christians, though it was ruthless and exceedingly cruel, was due, not to religious intolerance, but solely to political motives. There was reason to fear that the Christians might side with the King of Spain if he should attempt to conquer Japan; and even if no foreign power intervened, there was reason to fear rebellions of Christians against the newly established central power. Economic exploitation, in the modern sense of the word, did not yet exist apart from political domination, and the Japanese would have welcomed trade if there had been no danger of conquest. They seem to have overrated the power of Spain, which certainly could not have conquered them. Japanese armies were, in those days, far larger than the armies of Europe; the Japanese had learnt the use of fire-arms; and their knowledge of strategy was very great. Kyoto, the capital, was one of the largest cities in the world, having about a million inhabitants. The population of Japan was probably greater than that of any European State. It would therefore have been possible, without much trouble, to resist any expedition that Europe could have sent against Japan. It would even have been easy to conquer Manila, as Hideyoshi at one time thought of doing. But we can well understand how terrifying would be a map of the world showing the whole of North and South America as belonging to Philip II. Moreover the Japanese Government sent pretended converts to Europe, where they became priests, had audience of the Pope, penetrated into the inmost councils of Spain, and mastered all the meditated villainies of European Imperialism. These spies, when they came home and laid their reports before the Government, naturally increased its fears. The Japanese, therefore, decided to have no further intercourse with the white men. And whatever may be said against this policy, I cannot feel convinced that it was unwise.

For over two hundred years, until the coming of Commodore Perry's squadron from the United States in 1853, Japan enjoyed complete peace and almost complete stagnation—the only period of either in Japanese history. It then became necessary to learn fresh lessons in the use of fire-arms from Western nations, and to abandon the exclusive policy until they were learnt. When they have been learnt, perhaps we shall see another period of isolation.

## NOTES

1 The best book known to me on early Japan is Murdoch's *History of Japan*. The volume dealing with the earlier period is published by Kegan Paul, 1910. The chronologically later volume was published earlier; its title is: *A History of Japan during the Century of Early Foreign Intercourse* (1542–1651), by James Murdoch M.A. in collaboration with Isoh Yamagata. Kobe, office of the *Japan Chronicle*, 1903. I shall allude to these volumes as Murdoch I and Murdoch II respectively.
2 Murdoch I. pp. 113 ff.
3 Ibid., II. pp. 375 ff.
4 Murdoch I. p. 147.
5 Murdoch, II, p. 288.
6 Murdoch II, p. 667.

# 6

## MODERN JAPAN

The modern Japanese nation is unique, not only in this age, but in the history of the world. It combines elements which most Europeans would have supposed totally incompatible, and it has realized an original plan to a degree hardly known in human affairs. The Japan which now exists is almost exactly that which was intended by the leaders of the Restoration in 1867. Many unforeseen events have happened in the world: American has risen and Russia has fallen, China has become a Republic and the Great War has shattered Europe. But throughout all these changes the leading statesmen of Japan have gone along the road traced out for them at the beginning of the Meiji era, and the nation has followed them with ever-increasing faithfulness. One single purpose has animated leaders and followers alike: the strengthening and extension of the Empire. To realize this purpose a new kind of policy has been created, combining the sources of strength in modern America with those in Rome at the time of the Punic Wars, uniting the material organization and scientific knowledge of pre-war Germany with the outlook on life of the Hebrews in the Book of Joshua.

The transformation of Japan since 1867 is amazing, and people have been duly amazed by it. But what is still more amazing is that such an immense change in knowledge and in way of life should have brought so little change in religion and ethics, and that such change as it has brought in these matters should have been in a direction opposite to that which would have been naturally expected. Science is supposed to tend to rationalism; yet the spread of scientific knowledge in Japan has synchronized with a great intensification of Mikado worship, the most anachronistic feature in the Japanese civilization. For sociology, for social psychology, and for political theory, Japan is an extraordinarily interesting country. The synthesis of East and West which has been effected is of a most peculiar kind. There is far more of the East than appears on the surface; but there is everything of the West that tends to national efficiency. How far there is a genuine fusion of Eastern and Western elements may be doubted; the nervous excitability of the people suggests something strained and artificial in their way of life, but this may possibly be a merely temporary phenomenon.

Throughout Japanese politics since the Restoration, there are two separate strands, one analogous to that of Western nations, especially pre-war Germany, the other inherited from the feudal age, which is more analogous to the politics of the Scottish Highlands down to 1745. It is no part of my purpose to give a history of modern Japan; I wish only to give an outline of the forces which control events and movements in that country, with such illustrations as are necessary. There are many good books on Japanese politics; the one that I have found most informative is McLaren's *Political History of Japan during the Meiji Era 1867–1912* (Allen and Unwin, 1916). For a picture of Japan as it appeared in the early years of the Meiji era, Lafcadio Hearn is of course invaluable; his book *Japan, An Interpretation* shows his dawning realization of the grim sides of the Japanese character, after the cherry-blossom business has lost its novelty. I shall not have much to say about cherry-blossom; it was not flowering when I was in Japan.

Before 1867, Japan was a feudal federation of clans, in which the Central Government was in the hands of the Shogun, who was the head of his own clan, but had by no means undisputed sway over the more powerful of the other clans. There had been various dynasties of Shoguns at various times, but since the seventeenth century the Shogunate had been in the Tokugawa clan. Throughout the Tokugawa Shogunate, except during its first few years, Japan had been closed to foreign intercourse, except for a strictly limited commerce with the Dutch. The modern era was inaugurated by two changes: first, the compulsory opening of the country to Western trade; secondly, the transference of power from the Tokugawa clan to the clans of Satsuma and Choshu, who have governed Japan ever since. It is impossible to understand Japan or its politics and possibilities without realizing the nature of the governing forces and their roots in the feudal system of the former age. I will therefore first outline these internal movements, before coming to the part which Japan has played in international affairs.

What happened, nominally, in 1867 was that the Mikado was restored to power, after having been completely eclipsed by the Shogun since the end of the twelfth century. During this long period, the Mikado seems to have been regarded by the common people with reverence as a holy personage, but he was allowed no voice in affairs, was treated with contempt by the Shogun, was sometimes deposed if he misbehaved, and was often kept in great poverty.

Of so little importance was the Imperial person in the days of early foreign intercourse that the Jesuits hardly knew of the Emperor's existence. They seem to have thought of him as a Japanese counterpart of the Pope of Rome, except that he had no aspirations for temporal power. The Dutch writers likewise were in the habit of referring to the Shogun as "His Majesty," and on their annual pilgrimage from Dashima to Yedo, Kyoto (where the Mikado lived) was the only city which they were permitted to examine freely. The privilege was probably accorded by the Tokugawa to show the foreigners how lightly the Court was regarded. Commodore Perry delivered to the Shogun in Yedo the autograph letter to the Emperor of Japan from the President of the United States, and none of the Ambassadors of the Western

Powers seem to have entertained any suspicion that in dealing with the authorities in Yedo they were not approaching the throne.

In the light of these facts, some other explanation of the relations between the Shogunate and the Imperial Court must be sought than that which depends upon the claim now made by Japanese historians of the official type, that the throne, throughout this whole period, was divinely preserved by the Heavenly Gods.[1]

What happened, in outline, seems to have been a combination of very different forces. There were antiquarians who observed that the Mikado had had real power in the tenth century, and who wished to revert to the ancient customs. There were patriots who were annoyed with the Shogun for yielding to the pressure of the white men and concluding commercial treaties with them. And there were the western clans, which had never willingly submitted to the authority of the Shogun. To quote McLaren once more (p. 33):—

The movement to restore the Emperor was coupled with a form of Chauvinism or intense nationalism which may be summed up in the expression "Exalt the Emperor! Away with the barbarians!" (Kinno! Joi!) From this it would appear that the Dutch scholars[2] work in enlightening the nation upon the subject of foreign scientific attainments was anathema, but a conclusion of that kind must not be hastily arrived at. The cry, "Away with the barbarians!" was directed against Perry and the envoys of other foreign Powers, but there was nothing in that slogan which indicates a general unwillingness to emulate the foreigners' achievements in armaments or military tactics. In fact, for a number of years previous to 1853, Satsuma and Choshu and other western clans had been very busily engaged in manufacturing guns and practising gunnery: to that extent, at any rate, the discoveries of the students of European sciences had been deliberately used by those men who were to be foremost in the Restoration.

This passage gives the key to the spirit which has animated modern Japan down to the present day.

The Restoration was, to a greater extent than is usually realized in the West, a conservative and even reactionary movement. Professor Murdoch, in his authoritative *History of Japan*,[3] says:—

In the interpretation of this sudden and startling development most European writers and critics show themselves seriously at fault. Even some of the more intelligent among them find the solution of this portentous enigma in the very superficial and facile formula of "imitation." But the Japanese still retain their own unit of social organization, which is not the individual, as with us, but the *family*. Furthermore, the resemblance of the Japanese administrative system, both central and local, to certain European systems is not the result of imitation, or borrowing, or adaptation. Such resemblance is merely an odd and fortuitous resemblance. When the statesmen who overthrew the Tokugawa régime in 1868, and abolished the feudal system in 1871, were called upon to provide the nation with a new equipment of administrative machinery, they did not go to Europe for their models. They simply harked back for some eleven or twelve centuries in their own history and resuscitated the administrative machinery that had first been installed in Japan by the genius of Fujiwara Kamatari and his coadjutors in 645 A.D., and more fully supplemented and organized in the succeeding fifty or sixty years. The present Imperial Cabinet of ten Ministers, with their departments and departmental staff of officials, is a modified revival of the Eight Boards adapted from China and established in the seventh century. . . . The present administrative system is indeed of alien provenance; but it was neither borrowed nor adapted a generation ago, nor borrowed nor adapted from Europe. It was really a system of hoary antiquity that was revived to cope with pressing modern exigencies.

The outcome was that the clans of Satsuma and Choshu acquired control of the Mikado, made his exaltation the symbol of resistance to the foreigner (with whom the Shogun had concluded unpopular treaties), and secured the support of the country by being the champions of nationalism. Under extraordinarily able leaders, a policy was adopted which has been pursued consistently ever since, and has raised Japan from being the helpless victim of Western greed to being one of the greatest Powers in the world. Feudalism was abolished, the Central Government was made omnipotent, a powerful army and navy were created, China and Russia were successively defeated, Korea was annexed and a protectorate established over Manchuria and Inner Mongolia, industry and commerce were developed, universal compulsory education instituted, and worship of the Mikado firmly established by teaching in the schools and by professorial patronage of historical myths.

The artificial creation of Mikado-worship is one of the most interesting features of modern Japan, and a model to all other States as regards the method of preventing the growth of rationalism. There is a very instructive little pamphlet by Professor B. H. Chamberlain, who was Professor of Japanese and philosophy at Tokyo, and had a knowledge of Japanese which few Europeans had equalled. His pamphlet is called *The Invention of a New Religion*, and is published by the Rationalist Press Association. He points out that, until recent times, the religion of Japan was Buddhism, to the practical exclusion of every other. There had been, in very ancient times, a native religion called Shinto, and it had lingered on obscurely. But it is only during the last forty years or so that Shinto has been erected into a State religion, and has been reconstructed so as to suit modern requirements.[4] It is, of course, preferable to Buddhism because it is native and national; it is a tribal religion, not one which aims at appealing to all mankind. Its whole purpose, as it has been developed by modern statesmen, is to glorify Japan and the Mikado.

Professor Chamberlain points out how little reverence there was for the Mikado until some time after the Restoration:—

> The sober fact is that no nation probably has ever treated its sovereigns more cavalierly than the Japanese have done, from the beginning of authentic history down to within the memory of living men. Emperors have been deposed, emperors have been assassinated; for centuries every succession to the throne was the signal for intrigues

and sanguinary broils. Emperors have been exiled; some have been murdered in exile. . . . For long centuries the Government was in the hands of Mayors of the Palace, who substituted one infant sovereign for another, generally forcing each to abdicate as he approached man's estate. At one period, these Mayors of the Palace left the Descendant of the Sun in such distress that His Imperial Majesty and the Imperial Princes were obliged to gain a livelihood by selling their autographs! Nor did any great party in the State protest against this condition of affairs. Even in the present reign (that of Meiji)—the most glorious in Japanese history—there have been two rebellions, during one of which a rival Emperor was set up in one part of the country, and a Republic proclaimed in another.

This last sentence, though it states sober historical fact, is scarcely credible to those who only know twentieth-century Japan. The spread of superstition has gone *pari passu* with the spread of education, and a revolt against the Mikado is now unthinkable. Time and again, in the midst of political strife, the Mikado has been induced to intervene, and instantly the hottest combatants have submitted abjectly. Although there is a Diet, the Mikado is an absolute ruler—as absolute as any sovereign ever has been.

The civilization of Japan, before the Restoration, came from China. Religion, art, writing, philsophy and ethics, everything was copied from Chinese models. Japanese history begins in the fifth century A.D., whereas Chinese history goes back to about 2,000 B.C., or at any rate to somewhere in the second millennium B.C. This was galling to Japanese pride, so an early history was invented long ago, like the theory that the Romans were descended from Æneas. To quote Professor Chamberlain again :—

The first glimmer of genuine Japanese history dates from the fifth century *after* Christ, and even the accounts of what happened in the sixth century must be received with caution. Japanese scholars know this as well as we do; it is one of the certain results of investigation. But the Japanese bureaucracy does not desire to have the light let in on this inconvenient circumstance. While granting a dispensation *re* the national mythology, properly so called, it exacts belief in every iota of the national historic legends. Woe to the native professor who strays from the path of orthodoxy. His wife and children (and in Japan every man, however young, has a wife and children) will starve. From the late Prince Ito's grossly misleading *Commentary on the Japanese Constitution* down to school compendiums, the absurd dates are everywhere insisted upon.

This question of fictitious early history might be considered unimportant, like the fact that, with us, parsons have to pretend to believe the Bible, which some people think innocuous. But it is part of the whole system, which has a political object, to which free thought and free speech are ruthlessly sacrificed. As this same pamphlet says:—

Shinto, a primitive nature cult, which had fallen into discredit, was taken out of its cupboard and dusted. The common people, it is true, continued to place their affections on Buddhism, the popular festivals were Buddhist; Buddhist also the temples where they buried their dead. The governing class determined to change all this. They insisted on the Shinto doctrine that the Mikado descends in direct succession from the native Goddess of the Sun, and that He himself is a living God on earth who justly claims the absolute fealty of his subjects. Such things as laws and constitutions are but free gifts on His part, not in any sense popular rights. Of course, the ministers and officials, high and low, who carry on His government, are to be regarded not as public servants, but rather as executants of supreme—one might say supernatural—authority. Shinto, because connected with the Imperial family, is to be alone honoured.

All this is not mere theorizing; it is the practical basis of Japanese politics. The Mikado, after having been for centuries in the keeping of the Tokugawa Shoguns, was captured by the clans of Satsuma and Choshu, and has been in their keeping ever since. They were represented politically by five men, the Genro or Elder Statesmen, who are sometimes miscalled the Privy Council. Only two still survive. The Genro have no constitutional existence; they are merely the people who have the ear of the Mikado. They can make him say whatever they wish; therefore they are omnipotent. It has happened repeatedly that they have had against them the Diet and the whole force of public opinion; nevertheless they have invariably been able to enforce their will, because they could make the Mikado speak, and no one dare oppose the Mikado. They do not themselves take office; they select the Prime Minister and the Ministers of War and Marine, and allow them to bear the blame if anything goes wrong. The Genro are the real Government of Japan, and will presumably remain so until the Mikado is captured by some other clique.

From a patriotic point of view, the Genro have shown very great wisdom in the conduct of affairs. There is reason to think that if Japan were a democracy its policy would be more Chauvinistic than it is. Apologists of Japan, such as Mr. Bland, are in the habit of telling us that there is a Liberal anti-militarist party in Japan, which is soon going to dominate foreign policy. I see no reason to believe this. Undoubtedly there is a strong movement for increasing the power of the Diet and making the Cabinet responsible to it; there is also a feeling that the Ministers of War and Marine ought to be responsible to the Cabinet and the Prime Minister, not only to the Mikado directly.[5] But democracy in Japan does not mean a diminution of Chauvinism in foreign policy. There is a small Socialist party which is genuinely anti-Chauvinist and anti-militarist; this party, probably, will grow as Japanese industrialism grows. But so-called Japanese Liberals are just as Chauvinistic as the Government, and public opinion is more so. Indeed there have been occasions when the Genro, in spite of popular fury, has saved the nation from mistakes which it would certainly have committed if the Government had been democratic. One of the most interesting of these occasions was the conclusion of the Treaty of Portsmouth, after the Sino-Japanese war, which deserves to be told as illustrative of Japanese politics.[6]

In 1905, after the battles of Tsushima and Mukden, it became clear to impartial observers that Russia could accomplish nothing further at sea, and Japan could accomplish nothing further on land. The Russian Government was anxious to continue the war, having gradually accumulated men and stores in Manchuria, and greatly improved the working of the Siberian railway. The Japanese Government, on the contrary, knew that it had already achieved all the success it could hope for, and that it would be extremely difficult to raise the loans required for a prolongation of the war. Under these circumstances, Japan appealed secretly to President Roosevelt requesting his good offices for the restoration of peace. President Roosevelt therefore issued invitations to both belligerents to a peace conference. The Russian Government, faced by a strong peace party and incipient revolution, dared not refuse the invitation, especially in view of the fact that the sympathies of neutrals were on the whole with Japan. Japan, being anxious for peace, led Russia to suppose that Japan's demands would be so excessive as to alienate the sympathy of the world and afford a complete answer to the peace party in Russia. In particular, the Japanese gave out that they would absolutely insist upon an indemnity. The Government had in fact resolved, from the first, not to insist on an indemnity, but this was known to very few people in Japan, and to no one outside Japan. The Russians, believing that the Japanese would not give way about the indemnity, showed themselves generous as regards all other Japanese demands. To their horror and consternation, when they had already packed up and were just ready to break up the conference, the Japanese announced (as they had from the first intended to do) that they accepted the Russian concessions and would waive the claim to an indemnity. Thus the Russian Government and the Japanese people were alike furious, because they had been tricked—the former in the belief that it could yield everything except the indemnity without bringing peace, the latter in the belief that the Government would never give way about the indemnity. In Russia there was revolution; in Japan there were riots, furious diatribes in the Press, and a change of Government—of the nominal Government, that is to say, for the Genro continued to be the real power throughout. In this case, there is no doubt that the decision of the Genro to make peace was the right one from every point of view; there is also very little doubt that a peace advantageous to Japan could not have been made without trickery.

Foreigners unacquainted with Japan, knowing that there is a Diet in which the Lower House is elected, imagine that Japan is at least as democratic as prewar Germany. This is a delusion. It is true that Marquis Ito, who framed the Constitution, which was promulgated in 1889, took Germany for his model, as the Japanese have always done in all their Westernizing efforts, except as regards the Navy, in which Great Britain has been copied. But there were many points in which the Japanese Constitution differed from that of the German Empire. To begin with, the Reichstag was elected by manhood suffrage, whereas in Japan there is a property qualification which restricts the franchise to about 25 per cent of the adult males. This, however, is a small matter compared to the fact that the Mikado's power is far less limited than that of the Kaiser was. It is true that Japan does not differ from pre-war Germany in the fact that Ministers are not responsible to the Diet, but to the Emperor, and are responsible severally, not collectively. The War Minister must be a General, the Minister of Marine must be an Admiral; they take their orders, not from the Prime Minister, but from the military and naval authorities respectively, who, of course, are under the control of the Mikado. But in Germany the Reichstag had the power of the purse, whereas in Japan, if the Diet refuses to pass the Budget, the Budget of the previous year can be applied, and when the Diet is not sitting, laws can be enacted temporarily by Imperial decree—a provision which had no analogue in the German Constitution.

The Constitution having been granted by the Emperor of his free grace, it is considered impious to criticize it or to suggest any change in it, since this would imply that His Majesty's work was not wholly perfect. To understand the Constitution, it is necessary to read it in conjunction with the authoritative commentary of Marquis Ito, which was issued at the same time. Mr. Coleman very correctly summarizes the Constitution as follows[7]:—

Article I of the Japanese Constitution provides that "The Empire of Japan shall be reigned over and governed by a line of Emperors unbroken for ages eternal."

"By reigned over and governed," wrote Marquis Ito in his *Commentaries on the Constitution of Japan,* "it is meant that the Emperor on

His Throne combines in Himself the Sovereignty of the State and the Government of the country and of His subjects."

Article 3 of the Constitution states that "the Emperor is sacred and inviolable." Marquis Ito's comment in explanation of this is peculiarly Japanese. He says, "The Sacred Throne was established at the time when the heavens and earth became separated. The Empire is Heaven-descended, divine and sacred; He is pre-eminent above all His subjects. He must be reverenced and is inviolable. He has, indeed, to pay due respect to the law, but the law has no power to hold Him accountable to it. Not only shall there be no irreverence for the Emperor's person, but also shall He neither be made a topic of derogatory comment nor one of discussion."

Through the Constitution of Japan the Japanese Emperor exercises the legislative power, the executive power, and the judiciary power. The Emperor convokes the Imperial Diet, opens, closes, prorogues, and dissolves it. When the Imperial Diet is not sitting, Imperial ordinances may be issued in place of laws. The Emperor has supreme control of the Army and Navy, declares war, makes peace, and concludes treaties; orders amnesty, pardon and commutation of punishments.

As to the Ministers of State, the Constitution of Japan, Article 55, says: "The respective Ministers of State shall give their advice to the Emperor and be responsible for it."

Ito's commentary on this article indicates his intention in framing it. "When a Minister of State errs in the discharge of his functions, the power of deciding upon his responsibilities belongs to the Sovereign of the State: he alone can dismiss a Minister who has appointed him. Who then is it, except the Sovereign, that can appoint, dismiss, and punish a Minister of State? The appointment and dismissal of them having been included by the Constitution in the sovereign power of the Emperor, it is only a legitimate consequence that the power of deciding as to the responsibility of Ministers is withheld from the Diet. But the Diet may put questions to the Ministers and demand open answers from them before the public, and it may also present addresses to the Sovereign setting forth its opinions.

"The Minister President of State is to make representations to the Emperor on matters of State, and to indicate, according to His pleasure, the general course of the policy of the State, every branch of the administration being under control of the said Minister. The compass of his duties is large, and his responsibilities cannot but be proportionately great. As to the other Ministers of State, they are severally held responsible for the matters within their respective competency; there is no joint responsibility among them in regard to such matters. For, the Minister President and the other Ministers of State, being alike personally appointed by the Emperor, the proceedings of each one of them are, in every respect, controlled by the will of the Emperor, and the Minister President himself has no power of control over the posts occupied by other Ministers, while the latter ought not to be dependent upon the former. In some countries, the Cabinet is regarded as constituting a corporate body, and the Ministers are not held to take part in the conduct of the Government each one in an individual capacity, but joint responsibility is the rule. The evil of such a system is that the power of party combination will ultimately over-rule the supreme power of the Sovereign. Such a state of things can never be approved of according to our Constitution."

In spite of the small powers of the Diet, it succeeded, in the first four years of its existence (1890–94), in causing some annoyance to the Government. Until 1894, the policy of Japan was largely controlled by Marquis Ito, who was opposed to militarism and Chauvinism. The statesmen of the first half of the Meiji era were concerned mainly with introducing modern education and modern social organization; they wished to preserve Japanese independence vis-à-vis the Western Powers, but did not aim, for the time being, at imperialist expansion on their own account. Ito represented this older school of Restoration statesmen. Their ideas of statecraft were in the main derived from the Germany of the 'eighties, which was kept by Bismarck from undue adventurousness. But when the Diet proved difficult to manage, they reverted to an earlier phase of Bismarck's career for an example to imitate. The Prussian Landtag (incredible as it may seem) was vigorously obstreperous at the time when Bismarck first rose to power, but he tamed it by glutting the nation with military glory in the wars against Austria and France. Similarly, in 1894, the Japanese Government embarked on war against China, and instantly secured the enthusiastic support of the hitherto rebellious Diet. From that day to this, the Japanese Government has never been vigorously opposed except for its good deeds (such as the Treaty of Portsmouth); and it has atoned for these by abundant international crimes, which the nation has always applauded to the echo. Marquis Ito was responsible for the outbreak of war in 1894. He was afterwards again opposed to the new policy of predatory war, but was powerless to prevent it.[8] His opposition, however, was tiresome, until at last he was murdered in Korea.

Since the outbreak of the Sino-Japanese war in 1894, Japan has pursued a consistent career of imperialism, with quite extraordinary success. The nature and fruits of that career I shall consider in the next two chapters. For the time being, it has arrested whatever tendency existed towards the development of democracy; the Diet is quite as unimportant as the English Parliament was in the time of the Tudors. Whether the present system will continue for a long time, it is impossible to guess. An unsuccessful foreign war would probably destroy not only the existing system, but the whole unity and morale of the nation; I do not believe that Japan would be as firm in defeat as Germany has proved to be. Diplomatic failure, without war, would probably produce a more Liberal regime, without revolution. There is, however, one very explosive element in Japan, and that is industrialism. It is impossible for Japan to be a Great Power without developing her industry, and in fact everything possible is done to increase Japanese manufactures. Moreover, industry is required to absorb the growing population, which cannot emigrate to English-speaking regions, and will not emigrate to the mainland of Asia because Chinese competition is too severe. Therefore the only way to support a larger population is to absorb it into industrialism, manufacturing goods for export as a means of purchasing food abroad. Industrialism in Japan requires control of China, because Japan contains hardly any of the raw materials of industry, and cannot obtain them sufficiently cheaply or securely in open competition with America and Europe. Also dependence upon imported food requires a strong navy. Thus the motives for imperialism and navalism in Japan are very similar to those that have prevailed in England. But this policy requires high taxation, while successful competition in neutral markets requires— or rather, is thought to require—starvation wages and long hours for operatives. In the cotton industry of Osoka, for example, most of the work is done by girls under fourteen, who work eleven hours a day and got, in 1916, an average daily wage of 5d.[9] Labour organization is in its infancy, and so is Socialism;[10] but both are certain to spread if the number of industrial workers increases without a very marked improvement in hours and wages. Of course the very rigidity of the Japanese policy, which has given it its strength, makes it incapable of adjusting itself to Socialism and Trade Unionism, which are vigorously persecuted by the Government. And on the other hand Socialism and Trade Unionism cannot accept Mikado-worship and the whole farrago of myth upon which the Japanese State depends.[11] There is therefore a likelihood, some twenty or thirty years hence—assuming a peaceful and prosperous development in the meantime—of a very bitter class conflict between the proletarians on the one side and the employers and bureaucrats on the other. If this should happen to synchronize with agrarian discontent, it would be impossible to foretell the issue.

The problems facing Japan are therefore very difficult. To provide for the growing population it is necessary to develop industry; to develop industry it is necessary to control Chinese raw materials; to control Chinese raw materials it is necessary to go against the economic interests of America and Europe; to do this successfully requires a large army and navy, which in turn involve great poverty for wage-earners. And expanding industry with poverty for wage-earners means growing discontent, increase of Socialism, dissolution of filial piety and Mikado-worship in the poorer classes, and therefore a continually greater and greater menace to the whole foundation on which the fabric of the State is built. From without, Japan is threatened with the risk of war against America or of a revival of China. From within, there will be, before long, the risk of proletarian revolution.

From all these dangers, there is only one escape, and that is a diminution of the birth-rate. But such an idea is not merely abhorrent to the militarists as diminishing the supply of cannon-fodder; it is fundamentally opposed to Japanese religion and morality, of which patriotism and filial piety are the basis. Therefore if Japan is to emerge successfully, a much more intense Westernizing must take place, involving not only mechanical processes and knowledge of bare facts, but ideals and religion and general outlook on life. There must be free thought, scepticism, diminution in the intensity of herd-instinct. Without these, the population question cannot be solved; and if that remains unsolved, disaster is sooner or later inevitable.

## NOTES

1    McLaren, op. cit. p. 19.
2    Kegan Paul, 1910, vol. i. p. 20.
3    "What *popular* Shinto, as expounded by its village priests in the old time, was we simply do not know. Our carefully selected and edited official edition of Shinto is certainly not true aboriginal Shinto as practised in Yamato before the introduction of Buddhism and Chinese culture, and many plausible arguments which disregard that indubitable fact lose much of their weight." (Murdoch, I, p. 173 *n.*)
4    The strength of this movement may, however, be doubted. Murdoch (op. cit. i, p. 162) says: "At present, 1910, the War Office and Admiralty are, of all Ministries, by far the strongest in the Empire. When a party Government does by any strange hap make its appearance on the political stage, the Ministers of War and of Marine can afford to regard its advent with the utmost insouciance. For the most extreme of party politicians readily and unhesitatingly admit that the affairs of the Army and Navy do not fall within the sphere of party politics, but are the exclusive concern of the Commander-in-Chief, his Imperial Majesty the Emperor of Japan. On none in the public service of Japan are titles of nobility, high rank, and still more substantial emoluments showered with a more liberal hand than upon the great captains and the great sailors of the Empire. In China, on the other hand, the military man is, if not a pariah, at all events an exceptional barbarian, whom policy makes it advisable to treat with a certain amount of gracious, albeit semi-contemptuous, condescension."
5    The following account is taken from McLaren, op. cit. chaps. xii. and xiii.
6    *The Far East Unveiled*, pp. 252–53.
7    See McLaren, op. cit. pp. 227, 228, 289.
8    Coleman, op. cit. chap. xxxv.

9   See an invaluable pamphlet, "The Socialist and Labour Movements in Japan," published by the *Japan Chronicle*, 1921, for an account of what is happening in this direction.

10  *The Times* of February 7, 1922, contains a telegram from its correspondent in Tokyo, á *propos* of the funeral of Prince Yamagata, Chief of the Genro, to the following effect :—

"To-day a voice was heard in the Diet in opposition to the grant of expenses for the State funeral of Prince Yamagata. The resolution, which was introduced by the member for Osaka constituency, who is regarded as the spokesman of the so-called Parliamentary Labour Party founded last year, states that the Chief of the Genro (Elder Statesmen) did not render true service to the State, and, although the recipient of the highest dignities, was an enemy of mankind and suppressor of democratic institutions The outcome was a foregone conclusion, but the fact that the introducer could obtain the necessary support to table the resolution formally was not the least interesting feature of the incident."

# 7

# JAPAN AND CHINA BEFORE 1914

Before going into the detail of Japan's policy towards China, it is necessary to put the reader on his guard against the habit of thinking of the "Yellow Races," as though China and Japan formed some kind of unity. There are, of course, reasons which, at first sight, would lead one to suppose that China and Japan could be taken in one group in comparison with the races of Europe and of Africa. To begin with, the Chinese and Japanese are both yellow, which points to ethnic affinities; but the political and cultural importance of ethnic affinities is very small. The Japanese assert that the hairy Ainus, who are low in the scale of barbarians, are a white race akin to ourselves. I never saw a hairy Ainu, and I suspect the Japanese of malice in urging us to admit the Ainus as poor relations; but even if they really are of Aryan descent, that does not prove that they have anything of the slightest importance in common with us as compared to what the Japanese and Chinese have in common with us. Similarity of culture is infinitely more important than a common racial origin.

It is true that Japanese culture, until the Restoration, was derived from China. To this day, Japanese script is practically the same as Chinese, and Buddhism, which is still the religion of the people, is of the sort derived originally from China. Loyalty and filial piety, which are the foundations of Japanese ethics, are Confucian virtues, imported along with the rest of ancient Chinese culture. But even before the irruption of European influences, China and Japan had had such different histories and national temperaments that doctrines originally similar had developed in opposite directions. China has been, since the time of the First Emperor (c. 200 B.C.), a vast unified bureaucratic land empire, having much contact with foreign nations—Annamese, Burmese, Mongols, Tibetans and even Indians. Japan, on the other hand, was an island kingdom, having practically no foreign contact except with Korea and occasionally with China, divided into clans which were constantly at war with each other, developing the virtues and vices of feudal chivalry, but totally unconcerned with economic or administrative problems on a large scale. It was not difficult to adapt the doctrines of Confucius to such a country, because in the time of Confucius China was still feudal and still divided into a number of petty kingdoms, in one of which the sage himself was a courtier, like Goethe at Weimar. But naturally his doctrines underwent a different development from that which befel them in their own country.

In old Japan, for instance, loyalty to the clan chieftain is the virtue one finds most praised; it is this same virtue, with its scope enlarged, which has now become patriotism. Loyalty is a virtue naturally praised where conflicts between roughly equal forces are frequent, as they were in feudal Japan, and are in the modern international world. In China, on the contrary, power seemed so secure, the Empire was so vast and immemorial, that the need for loyalty was not felt. Security bred a different set of virtues, such as courtesy, considerateness, and compromise. Now that security is gone, and the Chinese find themselves plunged into a world of warring bandits, they have difficulty in developing the patriotism, ruthlessness, and unscrupulousness which the situation demands. The Japanese have no such difficulty, having been schooled for just such requirements by their centuries of feudal anarchy. Accordingly we find that Western influence has only accentuated the previous differences between China and Japan: modern Chinese like our thought but dislike our mechanism, while modern Japanese like our mechanism but dislike our thought.

From some points of view, Asia, including Russia, may be regarded as a unity; but from this unity Japan must be excluded. Russia, China, and India contain vast plains given over to peasant agriculture; they are easily swayed by military empires such as that of Jenghis Khan; with modern railways, they could be dominated from a centre more securely than in former times. They could be self-subsistent economically, and invulnerable to outside attack, independent of commerce, and so strong as to be indifferent to progress. All this may come about some day, if Russia happens to develop a great conqueror supported by German organizing ability. But Japan stands outside this order of possibilities. Japan, like Great Britain, must depend upon commerce for power and prosperity. As yet, Japan has not developed the Liberal mentality appropriate to a commercial nation, and is still bent upon Asiatic conquest and military prowess. This policy brings with it conflicts with China and Russia, which the present weakness of those Powers has enabled Japan, hitherto, to conduct successfully. But both are likely to recover their strength sooner or later, and then the essential weakness of present Japanese policy will become apparent.

It results naturally from the situation that the Japanese have two somewhat incompatible ambitions. On the one hand, they wish to pose as the champions of Asia against the oppression of the white man; on the other hand, they wish to be admitted to equality by the white Powers, and to join in the feast obtained by exploiting the nations that are inefficient in homicide. The former policy should make them friendly to China and India and hostile to the white races; the latter policy has inspired the Anglo-Japanese Alliance and its fruits in the annexation of Korea and the virtual annexation of Manchuria and Inner Mongolia. As a member of the League of Nations, of the Big Five at Versailles, and of the Big Three at Washington, Japan appears as one of the ordinary Great Powers; but at other moments Japan aims at establishing a hegemony in Asia by standing for the emancipation from white tyranny of those who happen to be yellow or brown, but not black. Count Okuma, speaking in the Kobe Chamber of Commerce, said: "There are three hundred million natives in India looking to us to rescue them from the thraldom of Great Britain."[1] While in the Far East, I inquired of innumerable Englishmen what advantage our Government could suppose that we derived from the Japanese Alliance. The only answer that seemed to me to supply an intelligible motive was that the Alliance somewhat mitigates the intensity of Japanese anti-British propaganda in India. However that may be, there can be no doubt that the Japanese would like to pose before the Indians as their champions against white tyranny. Mr. Pooley[2] quotes Dr. Ichimura of the Imperial University of Kyoto as giving the following list of white men's sins:—

(1)  White men consider that they alone are human beings, and that all coloured races belong to a lower order of civilization.
(2)  They are extremely selfish, insisting on their own interests, but ignoring the interests of all whom they regard as inferiors.
(3)  They are full of racial pride and conceit. If any concession is made to them they demand and take more.
(4)  They are extreme in everything, exceeding the coloured races in greatness and wickedness.
(5)  They worship money, and believing that money is the basis of everything, will adopt any measures to gain it.

This enumeration of our vices appears to me wholly just. One might have supposed that a nation which saw us in this light would endeavour to be unlike us. That, however, is not the moral which the Japanese draw. They argue, on the contrary, that it is necessary to imitate us as closely as possible. We shall find that, in the long catalogue of crimes committed by Europeans towards China, there is hardly one which has not been equalled by the Japanese. It never occurs to a Japanese, even in his wildest dreams, to think of a Chinaman as an equal. And although he wants the white man to regard himself as an equal, he himself regards Japan as immeasurably superior to any white country. His real desire is to be above the whites, not merely equal with them. Count Okuma put the matter very simply in an address given in 1913:—

> The white races regard the world as their property and all other races are greatly their inferiors. They presume to think that the rôle of the whites in the universe is to govern the world as they please. The Japanese were a people who suffered by this policy, and wrongfully, for the Japanese were not inferior to the white races, but fully their equals. The whites were defying destiny, and woe to them.[3]

It would be easy to quote statements by eminent men to the effect that Japan is the greatest of all nations. But the same could be said of the eminent men of all other nations down to Ecuador. It is the acts of the Japanese rather than their rhetoric that must concern us.

The Sino-Japanese war of 1894–5 concerned Korea, with whose internal affairs China and Japan had mutually agreed not to interfere without first consulting each other. The Japanese claimed that China had infringed this agreement. Neither side was in the right; it was a war caused by a conflict of rival imperialisms. The Chinese were easily and decisively defeated, and from that day to this have not ventured to oppose any foreign Power by force of arms, except unofficially in the Boxer rebellion. The Japanese were, however, prevented from reaping the fruits of their victory by the intervention of Russia, Germany and France, England holding aloof. The Russians coveted Korea for themselves, the French came in as their allies, and the Germans presumably joined them because of William H's dread of the Yellow Peril. However that may be, this intervention made the Russo-Japanese war inevitable. It would not have mattered much to Japan if the Chinese had established themselves in Korea, but the Russians would have constituted a serious menace. The Russians did not befriend China for nothing; they acquired a lease of Port Arthur and Dalny (now called Dairen), with railway and mining rights in Manchuria. They built the Chinese Eastern Railway, running right through Manchuria, connecting Port Arthur and Peking with the Siberian Railway and Europe. Having accomplished all this, they set to work to penetrate Korea.

The Russo-Japanese war would presumably not have taken place but for the Anglo-Japanese Alliance, concluded in 1902. In British policy, this Alliance has always had a somewhat minor place, while it has been the corner-stone of Japanese foreign policy, except during the Great War, when the Japanese thought that Germany would win. The Alliance provided that, in the event of either Power being attacked by two Powers at once, the other should come to its assistance. It was, of course, originally inspired by fear of Russia, and was framed with a view to preventing the Russian Government, in the event of war with Japan or England, from calling upon the help of France. In 1902 we were hostile to France and Russia, and Japan remained hostile to Russia until after the Treaty of Portsmouth had been supplemented by the Convention of 1907. The Alliance served its purpose admirably for both parties during the Russo-Japanese war. It kept France from joining Russia, and thereby enabled Japan to acquire command of the sea. It enabled Japan to weaken Russia, thus curbing Russian ambitions, and making it possible for us to conclude an Entente with Russia in 1907. Without this Entente, the Entente concluded with France in 1904 would have been useless, and the alliance which defeated Germany could not have been created.

Without the Anglo-Japanese Alliance, Japan could not have fought Russia alone, but would have had to fight France also. This was beyond her strength at that time. Thus the decisive step in Japan's rise to greatness was due to our support.

The war ended with a qualified victory for Japan. Russia renounced all interference in Korea, surrendered Port Arthur and Dalny (since called Dairen) to the Japanese, and also the railway as far north as Changchun. This part of the railway, with a few branch lines, has since then been called the South Manchurian Railway. From Dairen to Changchun is 437 miles; Changchun is 150 miles south of Harbin. The Japanese use Dairen as the commercial port for Manchuria, reserving Port Arthur for purely naval purposes. In regard to Korea, Japan has conformed strictly to Western models. During the Russo-Japanese war, the Japanese made a treaty guaranteeing the independence and integrity of Korea; in 1910 they annexed Korea; since then they have suppressed Korean nationalists with every imaginable severity. All this establishes their claim to be fully the equals of the white men.

The Japanese not merely hold the South Manchurian Railway, but have a monopoly of railway construction in South Manchuria. As this was practically the beginning of Japan's control of large regions in China by means of railways monopolies, it will be worth while to quote Mr. Pooley's account of the Fa-ku-Men Railway incident,[4] which shows how the South Manchurian monopoly was acquired:—

"In November 1907 the Chinese Government signed a contract with Messrs Pauling and Co. for an extension of the Imperial Chinese railways northwards from Hsin-min-Tung to Fa-ku-Men, the necessary capital for the work being found by the British and Chinese Corporation. Japan protested against the contract, firstly, on an alleged secret protocol annexed to the treaty of Peking, which was alleged to have said that ' the Chinese Government shall not construct any main line in the neighbourhood of or parallel to the South Manchurian Railway, nor any branch line which should be prejudicial to the interests of that railway '; and, secondly, on the Convention of 1902, between China and Russia, that no railway should be built from Hsin-min-Tung without Russian consent. As by the Treaty of Portsmouth, Japan succeeded to the Russian rights, the projected line could not be built without her consent. Her diplomatic communications were exceedingly offensive in tone, and concluded with a notification that, if she was wrong, it was obviously only Russia who could rightfully take her to task!

"The Chinese Government based its action in granting the contract on the clause of the 1898 contract for the construction of the Chung-hon-so to Hsin-min-Tung line, under which China specifically reserved the right to build the Fa-ku-Men line with the aid of the same contractors. Further, although by the Russo-British Note of 1898 British subjects were specifically excluded from participation in railway construction north of the Great Wall, by the Additional Note attached to the Russo-British Note the engagements between the Chinese Government and the British and Chinese Corporation were specifically reserved from the purview of the agreement.

"Even if Japan, as the heir of Russia's assets and liabilities in Manchuria, had been justified in her protest by the Convention of 1902 and by the Russo-British Note of 1899, she had not fulfilled her part of the bargain, namely, the Russian undertaking in the Note to abstain from seeking concession, rights and privileges in the valley of the Yangtze. Her reliance on the secret treaty carried weight with Great Britain, but with no one else, as may be gauged from the records of the State Department at Washington. A later claim advanced by Japan that her action was justified by Article VI of the Treaty of Portsmouth, which assigned to Japan all Russian rights in the Chinese Eastern Railway (South Manchurian Railway) 'with all rights and properties appertaining thereto,' was effectively answered by China's citation of Articles III and IV of the same Treaty. Under the first of these articles it is declared that 'Russia has no territorial advantages or preferential or exclusive concessions in Manchuria in impairment of Chinese sovereignty or inconsistent with the principle of equal opportunity'; whilst the second is a reciprocal engagement by Russia and Japan 'not to obstruct any general measures common to all countries which China may take for the development of the commerce and industry of Manchuria.'

"It would be interesting to know whether a refusal to allow China to build a railway on her own territory is or is not an impairment of Chinese sovereignty and whether such a railway as that proposed was not a measure for the 'development of the commerce and industry of Manchuria."

"It is doubtful if even the Russo-Japanese war created as much feeling in China as did the Fa-ku-men incident. Japan's action was of such flagrant dishonesty and such a cynical repudiation of her promises and pledges that her credit received a blow from which it has never since recovered. The abject failure of the British Government to support its subjects' treaty rights was almost as much an eye-opener to the world as the protest from Tokio….

"The methods which had proved so successful in stopping the Fa-ku-men railway were equally successful in forcing the abandonment of other projected railways. Among these were the Chin-chou-Aigun line and the important Antung-Mukden line.[5] The same alleged secret protocol was used equally brutally and successfully for the acquisition of the Newchwang line, and participation in 1909, and eventual acquisition in 1914, of the Chan-Chun-Kirin lines. Subsequently by an agreement with Russia the sixth article of the Russo-Chinese Agreement of 1896 was construed to mean 'the absolute and exclusive rights of administration within the railway zone.'"

Japan's spheres of influence have been subsequently extended to cover the whole of Manchuria and the whole of Shantung—though the latter has been nominally renounced at Washington. By such methods as the above, or by loans to impecunious Chinese authorities, the Japanese have acquired vast railway monopolies wherever their influence has penetrated, and have used the railways as a means of acquiring all real power in the provinces through which they run.

After the Russo-Japanese war, Russia and Japan became firm friends, and agreed to bring pressure on China jointly in any matter affecting Manchuria. Their friendship lasted until the Bolshevik revolution. Russia had entered into extensive obligations to support Japan's claims at the Peace Conference, which of course the Bolsheviks repudiated. Hence the implacable hostility of Japan to Soviet Russia, leading to the support of innumerable White filibusters in the territory of the Far Eastern Republic, and to friendship with France in all international questions.

As soon as there began to be in China a revolutionary party aiming at the overthrow of the Manchus, the Japanese supported it. They have continuously supported either or both sides in Chinese dissensions, as they judged most useful for prolonging civil war and weakening China politically. Before the revolution of 1911, Sun Yat Sen was several times in Japan, and there is evidence that as early as 1900 he was obtaining financial support from some Japanese.[6] When the revolution actually broke out, Japan endeavoured to support the Manchus, but was prevented from doing so effectively by the other Legations. It seems that the policy of Japan at that time, as later, was to prevent the union of North and South, and to confine the revolution to the South. Moreover, reverence for monarchy made Japan unwilling to see the Emperor of China dispossessed and his whole country turned into a

Republic, though it would have been agreeable to see him weakened by the loss of some southern provinces. Mr. Pooley gives a good account of the actions of Japan during the Chinese Revolution, of which the following quotation gives the gist[7]:—

It [the Genro] commenced with a statement from Prince Katsura on December 18th [1911], that the time for intervention had arrived, with the usual rider "for the sake of the peace of the Far East." This was followed by a private instruction to M. Ijuin, Japanese Minister in Peking, where-under the latter on December 23rd categorically informed Yuan-shi-kai that under no circumstances would Japan recognize a republican form of government in China.... In connection with the peace conference held at Shanghai, Mr. Matsui (now Japanese Ambassador to France), a trusted Councillor of the Foreign Office, was dispatched to Peking to back M. Ijuin in the negotiations to uphold the dynasty. Simultaneously, Mr. Denison, Legal Adviser to the Japanese Foreign Office, was sent to Shanghai to negotiate with the rebel leaders. Mr. Matsui's mission was to bargain for Japanese support of the Manchus against the rebels, Manchuria against the throne; Mr. Denison's mission was to bargain for Japanese support of the rebels against the throne, recognition by Peking of the Southern Republic against virtually a Japanese protectorate of that Republic and exclusive railway and mining concessions within its borders. The rebels absolutely refused Mr. Denison's offer, and sent the proposed terms to the Russian Minister at Peking, through whom they eventually saw the light of day. Needless to say the Japanese authorities strenuously denied their authenticity.

The British Legation, however, supported Yuan Shi-k'ai, against both the Manchus and Sun Yat Sen; and it was the British policy which won the day. Yuan Shi-k'ai became President, and remained so until 1915. He was strongly anti-Japanese, and had, on that ground, been opposed as strongly as Japan dared. His success was therefore a blow to the influence of Japan in China. If the Western Powers had remained free to make themselves felt in the Far East, the course of events would doubtless have been much less favourable to the Japanese; but the war came, and the Japanese saw their chance. How they used it must be told in a separate chapter.

## NOTES

1 Quoted by A. M. Pooley, *Japan's Foreign Policy*, Allen & Unwin, 1920, p. 18.
2 Op. cit. p. 16 n.
3 Pooley, op. cit. p. 17.
4 A. M. Pooley, *Japan's Foreign Policies*, pp. 48–51.
5 This line was subsequently built by the Japanese.
6 Pooley, op. cit., pp. 57–8.
7 Page 66.

# 8

## JAPAN AND CHINA DURING THE WAR

The most urgent problem in China's relations with foreign powers is Japanese aggression. Originally Japan was less powerful than China, but after 1868 the Japanese rapidly learnt from us whatever we had to teach in the way of skilful homicide, and in 1894 they resolved to test their new armaments upon China, just as Bismarck tested his on Denmark. The Chinese Government preserved its traditional haughtiness, and appears to have been quite unaware of the defeat in store for it. The question at issue was Korea, over which both Powers claimed suzerainty. At that time there would have been no reason for an impartial neutral to take one side rather than the other. The Japanese were quickly and completely victorious, but were obliged to fight Russia before obtaining secure possession of Korea. The war with Russia (1904–5) was fought chiefly in Manchuria, which the Russians had gained as a reward for befriending China. Port Arthur and Southern

Manchuria up to Mukden were acquired by the Japanese as a result of the Russo-Japanese war; the rest of Manchuria came under Japanese control as a result of Russia's collapse after the Great War.

The nominal sovereignty in Manchuria is still Chinese; the Chinese have the civil administration, an army, and the appointment of the Viceroy. But the Japanese also have troops in Manchuria; they have the railways, the industrial enterprises, and the complete economic and military control. The Chinese Viceroy could not remain in power a week if he were displeasing to the Japanese, which, however, he takes care not to be. (See Note A.) The same situation was being brought about in Shantung.

Shantung brings us to what Japan did in the Great War. In 1914, China could easily have been induced to join the Allies and to set to work to turn the Germans out of Kiao-Chow, but this did not suit the Japanese, who undertook the work themselves and insisted upon the Chinese remaining neutral (until 1917). Having captured Tsing-tau, they presented to the Chinese the famous Twenty-One Demands, which gave the Chinese Question its modern form. These demands, as originally presented in January 1915, consisted of five groups. The first dealt with Shantung, demanding that China should agree in advance to whatever terms Japan might ultimately make with Germany as regarded this Chinese province, that the Japanese should have the right to construct certain specified railways, and that certain ports (unspecified) should be opened to trade; also that no privileges in Shantung should be granted to any Power other than Japan. The second group concerns South Manchuria and Eastern Inner Mongolia, and demands what is in effect a protectorate, with control of railways, complete economic freedom for Japanese enterprise, and exclusion of all other foreign industrial enterprise. The third group gives Japan a monopoly of the mines and iron and steel works in a certain region of the Yangtze,[1] where we claim a sphere of influence. The fourth group consists of a single demand, that China shall not cede any harbour, bay or island to any Power except Japan. The fifth group, which was the most serious, demanded that Japanese political, financial, and military advisers should be employed by the Chinese Government; that the police in important places should be administered by Chinese and Japanese jointly, and should be largely Japanese in *personnel*; that China should purchase from Japan at least 50 per cent of her munitions, or obtain them from a Sino-Japanese arsenal to be established in China, controlled by Japanese experts and employing Japanese material; that Japan should have the right to construct certain railways in and near the Yangtze valley; that Japan should have industrial priority in Fukien (opposite Formosa); and finally that the Japanese should have the right of missionary propaganda in China, to spread the knowledge of their admirable ethics.

These demands involved, as is obvious, a complete loss of Chinese independence, the closing of important areas to the commerce and industry of Europe and America, and a special attack upon the British position in the Yangtze. We, however, were so busy with the war that we had no time to think of keeping ourselves alive. Although the demands constituted a grave menace to our trade, although the Far East was in an uproar about them, although America took drastic diplomatic action against them, Mr. Lloyd George never heard of them until they were explained to him by the Chinese Delegation at Versailles.[2] He had no time to find out what Japan wanted, but had time to conclude a secret agreement with Japan in February 1917, promising that whatever Japan wanted in Shantung we would support at the Peace Conference.[3] By the terms of the Anglo-Japanese Alliance, Japan was bound to communicate the Twenty-one Demands to the British Government. In fact, Japan communicated the first four groups, but not the fifth and worst, thus definitely breaking the treaty;[4] but this also, one must suppose, Mr. Lloyd George only discovered by chance when he got to Versailles.

China negotiated with Japan about the Twenty-one Demands, and secured certain modifications, but was finally compelled to yield by an ultimatum. There was a modification as regards the Hanyehping mines on the Yangtze, presumably to please us; and the specially obnoxious fifth group was altered into an exchange of studiously vague Notes.[5] In this form, the demands were accepted by China on May 9, 1915. The United States immediately notified Japan that they could not recognize the agreement. At that time America was still neutral, and was therefore still able to do something to further the objects for which we were supposed to be fighting, such as protection of the weaker nations. In 1917, however, after America had entered the war for self-determination, it became necessary to placate Japan, and in November of that year the Ishii-Lansing Agreement was concluded, by which "the Government of the United States recognizes that Japan has special interests in China, particularly for the parts to which her possessions are contiguous." The rest of the agreement (which is long) consists of empty verbiage.[6]

I come now to the events leading up to China's entry into the war.[7] In this matter, the lead was taken by America so far as severing diplomatic relations was concerned, but passed to Japan as regards the declaration of war. It will be remembered that, when America broke off diplomatic relations with Germany, President Wilson called upon all neutrals to do likewise. Dr. Paul S. Reinsch, United States Minister in Peking, proceeded to act with vigour in accordance with this policy. He induced China first, on February 9, 1917, to send a Note of expostulation to Germany on the subject of the submarine campaign; then, on March 14th, to break off diplomatic relations. The further step of declaring war was not taken until August 14th. The intrigues connected with these events deserve some study.

In view of the fact that the Japanese were among the Allies, the Chinese had not any strong tendency to take sides against Germany. The English, French and Russians had always desired the participation of China (for reasons which I shall explain presently), and there appears to have been some suggestion, in the early days of the war, that China should participate in return for our recognizing Yuan Shi-k'ai as Emperor. These suggestions, however, fell through owing to the opposition of Japan, based partly on hostility to Yuan Shi-k'ai, partly on the fear that China would be protected by the Allies if she became a belligerent. When, in November 1915, the British, French and Russian Ambassadors in Tokyo requested Japan to join in urging China to join the Allies, Viscount Ishii said that "Japan considered developments in China as of paramount interest to her, and she must keep a firm hand there. Japan could not regard with equanimity the organization of an efficient Chinese army such as would be required for her active participation in the war, nor could Japan fail to regard with uneasiness a liberation of the economic activities of 400,000,000 people."[8] Accordingly the proposal lapsed. It must be understood that throughout the war the Japanese were in a position to blackmail the Allies, because their sympathies were with Germany, they believed Germany would win, and they filled their newspapers with scurrilous attacks on the British, accusing them of cowardice and military incompetence.[9]

But when America severed diplomatic relations with Germany, the situation for China was changed. America was not bound to subservience to Japan, as we were; America was not one of the Allies; and America had always been China's best friend. Accordingly, the Chinese were willing to take the advice of America, and proceeded to sever diplomatic relations with Germany in March 1917. Dr. Reinsch was careful to make no promises to the Chinese, but of course he held out hopes. The American Government, at that time, could honestly hold out hopes, because it was ignorant of the secret treaties and agreements by which the Allies were bound. The Allies, however, can offer no such excuse for having urged China to take the further step of declaring war. Russia, France, and Great Britain had all sold China's rights to secure the continued support of Japan.

In May 1916, the Japanese represented to the Russians that Germany was inviting Japan to make a separate peace. In July 1916, Russia and Japan concluded a secret treaty, subsequently published by the Bolsheviks. This treaty constituted a separate alliance, binding each to come to the assistance of the other in any war, and recognizing that "the vital interests of one and the other of them require the safeguarding of China from the political domination of any third Power whatsoever, having hostile designs against Russia or Japan." The last article provided that "the present agreement must remain profoundly secret except to both of the High Contracting Parties."[10] That is to say, the treaty was not communicated to the other Allies, or even to Great Britain, in spite of Article 3 of the Anglo-Japanese Alliance, which provides that "The High Contracting Parties agree that neither of them will, without consulting the other, enter into a separate agreement with another Power to the prejudice of the objects described in the preamble of this Agreement," one of which objects was the preservation of equal opportunity for all Powers in China and of the independence and integrity of the Chinese Empire.

On February 16, 1917, at the very time when America was urging China to sever diplomatic relations with Germany, we concluded an agreement with Japan containing the following words:—

> His Britannic Majesty's Government accedes with pleasure to the request of the Japanese Government for an assurance that they will support Japan's claims in regard to the disposal of Germany's rights in Shantung and possessions in the islands north of the equator on the occasion of the Peace Conference; it being understood that the Japanese Government will, in the eventual peace settlement, treat in the same spirit Great Britain's claims to the German islands south of the equator.

The French attitude about Shantung, at the same time, is indicated by Notes which passed between France and Japan at Tokyo.[11] On February 19th, Baron Motono sent a communication to the French and Russian Ambassadors stating, among other things, that "the Imperial Japanese Government proposes to demand from Germany at the time of the peace negotiations, the surrender of the territorial rights and special interests Germany possessed before the war in Shantung and the islands belonging to her situated north of the equator in the Pacific Ocean." The French Ambassador, on March 2nd, replied as follows:—

> The Government of the French Republic is disposed to give the Japanese Government its accord in regulating at the time of the Peace Negotiations questions vital to Japan concerning Shantung and the German islands on the Pacific north of the equator. It also agrees to support the demands of the Imperial Japanese Government for the surrender of the rights Germany possessed before the war in this Chinese province and these islands.

M. Briand demands on the other hand that Japan give its support to obtain from China the breaking of its diplomatic relations with Germany, and that it give this act desirable significance. The consequences in China should be the following:

First, handing passports to the German diplomatic agents and consuls;

Second, the obligation of all under German jurisdiction to leave Chinese territory;

Third, the internment of German ships in Chinese ports and the ultimate requisition of these ships in order to place them at the disposition of the Allies, following the example of Italy and Portugal;

Fourth, requisition of German commercial houses, established in China; forfeiting the rights of Germany in the concessions she possesses in certain ports of China.

The Russian reply to Baron Motono's Note to the French and Russian Ambassadors, dated March 5, 1917, was as follows:—

In reply to the Note of the Japanese Ministry of Foreign Affairs, under the date of February 19th last, the Russian Embassy is charged with giving the Japanese Government the assurance that it can entirely count on the support of the Imperial Government of Russia with regard to its desiderata concerning the eventual surrender to Japan of the rights belonging to Germany in Shantung and of the German Islands, occupied by the Japanese forces, in the Pacific Ocean to the north of the Equator.[12]

It will be observed that, unlike England and France, Russia demands no quid pro quo, doubtless owing to the secret treaty concluded in the previous year.

After these agreements, Japan saw no further objection to China's participation in the war. The chief inducement held out to China was the hope of recovering Shantung; but as there was now no danger of this hope being realized, Japan was willing that America, in more or less honest ignorance, should unofficially use this hope for the persuasion of the Chinese. It is true that Japan had reason to fear America until the last days of the Peace Conference, but this fear was considerably diminished by the conclusion of the Lansing-Ishii Agreement in November 1917.

Meanwhile Japan had discovered that the question of China's entry into the war could be used to increase internal strife in China, which has been one of the aims of Japanese policy ever since the beginning of the revolutionary movement.[13] If the Chinese had not been interfered with at this time, there was some prospect of their succeeding in establishing a stable democratic government. Yuan was dead, and his successor in the Presidency, Li Yuan Hung, was a genuine constitutionalist. He reassembled the Parliament which Yuan had dismissed, and the work of drafting a permanent constitution was resumed. The President was opposed to severing diplomatic relations, and, of course, still more to declaring war. The Prime Minister, Tuan Chih-jui, a militarist, was strongly in favour of war. He and his Cabinet persuaded a considerable majority of both Houses of the Chinese Parliament to side with them on the question of severing diplomatic relations, and the President, as in duty bound, gave way on this issue.

On the issue of declaring war, however, public opinion was different. It was President Wilson's summons to the neutrals to follow him in breaking off diplomatic relations that had given force to the earlier campaign; but on June 5th the American Minister, acting on instructions, presented a Note to the Chinese Government urging that the preservation of national unity was more important than entry into the war, and suggesting the desirability of preserving peace for the present. What had happened in the meantime was that the war issue, which might never have become acute but for President Wilson's action, had been used by the Japanese to revive the conflict between North and South, and to instigate the Chinese militarists to unconstitutional action. Sun Yat Sen and most of the Southern politicians were opposed to the declaration of war; Sun's reasons were made known in an open letter to Mr. Lloyd George on March 7th. They were thoroughly sound.[14]

The Cabinet, on May 1st, decided in favour of war, but by the Constitution a declaration of war required the consent of Parliament. The militarists attempted to coerce Parliament, which had a majority against war; but as this proved impossible, they brought military force to bear on the President to compel him to dissolve Parliament unconstitutionally. The bulk of the Members of Parliament retired to the South, where they continued to act as a Parliament and to regard themselves as the sole source of constitutional government. After these various illegalities, the military autocrats were still compelled to deal with one of their number, who, in July, effected a five days' restoration of the Manchu Emperor. The President resigned, and was succeeded by a person more agreeable to the militarists, who have henceforth governed in the North, sometimes without a Parliament, sometimes with a subservient unconstitutional Northern Parliament. Then at last they were free to declare war. It was thus that China entered the war for democracy and against militarism.

Of course China helped little, if at all, towards the winning of the war, but that was not what the Allies expected of her. The objects of the European Allies are disclosed in the French Note quoted above. We wished to confiscate German property in China, to expel Germans living in China, and to prevent, as far as possible, the revival of German trade in China after the war. The confiscation of German property was duly carried out—not only public property, but private property also, so that the Germans in China were suddenly reduced to beggary. Owing to the claims on shipping, the expulsion of the Germans had to wait till after the Armistice. They were sent home through the Tropics in overcrowded ships, sometimes with only 24 hours' notice; no degree of hardship was sufficient to secure exemption. The British authorities insisted on expelling delicate pregnant women, whom they officially knew to be very likely to die on the voyage. All this was done after the Armistice, for the sake of British trade. The kindly Chinese often took upon themselves to hide Germans, in hard cases, from the merciless persecution of the Allies; otherwise, the miseries inflicted would have been much greater.

The confiscation of private property during the war and by the Treaty of Versailles was a new departure, showing that on this point all the belligerents agreed with the Bolsheviks. Dr. Reid places side by side two statements, one by President Wilson when asking Congress to agree to the Declaration of War: "We shall, I feel confident, conduct our operations as belligerents without passion, and ourselves observe with proud punctilio the principles of right and fairplay we profess to be fighting for"; the other by Senator Hitchcock, when the war was over, after a day spent with President Wilson in learning the case for ratification of the Versailles Treaty: "Through the Treaty, we will yet get very much of importance. . . . In violation of all international law and treaties we have made disposition of a billion dollars of German-owned property here. The Treaty validates all that."[15] The European Allies secured very similar advantages from inducing China to enter the war for righteousness.

We have seen what England and France gained by the Chinese declaration of war. What Japan gained was somewhat different.

The Northern military faction, which controlled the Peking Government, was completely dependent upon Japan, and could do nothing to resist Japanese aggression. All the other Powers were fully occupied with the war, and had sold China to Japan in return for Japanese neutrality—for Japan can hardly be counted as a belligerent after the capture of Tsingtau in November 1914. The Southern Government and all the liberal elements in the North were against the clique which had seized the Central Government. In March 1918, military and naval agreements were concluded between China and Japan, of which the text, never officially published, is given by Millard.[16] By these agreements the Japanese were enabled, under pretence of military needs in Manchuria and Mongolia, to send troops into Chinese territory, to acquire control of the Chinese Eastern Railway and consequently of Northern Manchuria, and generally to keep all Northern China at their mercy. In all this, the excuse of operations against the Bolsheviks was very convenient.

After this the Japanese went ahead gaily. During the year 1918, they placed loans in China to the extent of Yen 246,000,000,[17] i.e., about

£25,000,000. China was engaged in civil war, and both sides were as willing as the European belligerents to sell freedom for the sake of victory. Unfortunately for Japan, the side on which Japan was fighting in the war proved suddenly victorious, and some portion of the energies of Europe and America became available for holding Japan in check. For various reasons, however, the effect of this did not show itself until after the Treaty of Versailles was concluded. During the peace negotiations, England and France, in virtue of secret agreements, were compelled to support Japan. President Wilson, as usual, sacrificed everything to his League of Nations, which the Japanese would not have joined unless they had been allowed to keep Shantung. The chapter on this subject in Mr. Lansing's account of the negotiations is one of the most interesting in his book.[18] By Article 156 of the Treaty of Versailles, "Germany renounces, in favour of Japan, all her rights, title, and privileges" in the province of Shantung.[19] Although President Wilson had consented to this gross violation of justice, America refused to ratify the Treaty, and was therefore free to raise the issue of Shantung at Washington. The Chinese delegates at Versailles resisted the clauses concerning Shantung to the last, and finally, encouraged by a vigorous agitation of Young China,[20] refused to sign the Treaty. They saw no reason why they should be robbed of a province as a reward for having joined the Allies. All the other Allies agreed to a proceeding exactly as iniquitous as it would have been if we had annexed Virginia as a reward to the Americans for having helped us in the war, or France had annexed Kent on a similar pretext.

Meanwhile, Young China had discovered that it could move Chinese public opinion on the anti-Japanese cry. The Government in Peking in 1919–20 was in the hands of the pro-Japanese An Fu party, but they were forcibly ejected, in the summer of 1920, largely owing to the influence of the Young China agitation on the soldiers stationed in Peking. The An Fu leaders took refuge in the Japanese Legation, and since then the Peking Government has ventured to be less subservient to Japan, hoping always for American support. Japan did everything possible to consolidate her position in Shantung, but always with the knowledge that America might re-open the question at any time.

As soon as the Washington Conference was announced, Japan began feverishly negotiating with China, with a view to having the question settled before the opening of the Conference. But the Chinese, very wisely, refused the illusory concessions offered by Japan, and insisted on almost unconditional evacuation. At Washington, both parties agreed to the joint mediation of England and America. The pressure of American public opinion caused the American Administration to stand firm on the question of Shantung, and I understand that the British delegation, on the whole, concurred with America. Some concessions were made to Japan, but they will not amount to much if American interest in Shantung lasts for another five years. On this subject, I shall have more to say when I come to the Washington Conference.

There is a question with which the Washington Conference determined not to concern itself, but which nevertheless is likely to prove of great importance in the Far East—I mean the question of Russia. It was considered good form in diplomatic circles, until the Genoa Conference, to pretend that there is no such country as Russia, but the Bolsheviks, with their usual wickedness, have refused to fall in with this pretence. Their existence constitutes an embarrassment to America, because in a quarrel with Japan the United States would unavoidably find themselves in unwilling alliance with Russia. The conduct of Japan towards Russia has been quite as bad as that of any other Power. At the time of the Czecho-Slovak revolt, the Allies jointly occupied Vladivostok, but after a time all withdrew except the Japanese. All Siberia east of Lake Baikal, including Vladivostok, now forms one State, the Far Eastern Republic, with its capital at Chita. Against this Republic, which is practically though not theoretically Bolshevik, the Japanese have launched a whole series of miniature Kolchaks—Semenov, Horvath, Ungern, etc. These have all been defeated, but the Japanese remain in military occupation of Vladivostok and a great part of the Maritime Province, though they continually affirm their earnest wish to retire.

In the early days of the Bolshevik régime the Russians lost Northern Manchuria, which is now controlled by Japan. A board consisting partly of Chinese and partly of reactionary Russians forms the directorate of the Chinese Eastern Railway, which runs through Manchuria and connects with the Siberian Railway. There is no through communication by rail between Peking and Europe as in the days before 1914. This is an extreme annoyance to European business men in the Far East, since it means that letters or journeys from Peking to London take five or six weeks instead of a fortnight. They try to persuade themselves that the fault lies with the Bolsheviks, but they are gradually realizing that the real cause is the reactionary control of the Chinese Eastern Railway. Meanwhile, various Americans are interesting themselves in this railway and endeavouring to get it internationalized. Motives similar to those which led to the Vanderlip concession are forcing friendship with Russia upon all Americans who have Siberian interests. If Japan were engaged in a war with America, the Bolsheviks would in all likelihood seize the opportunity to liberate Vladivostok and recover Russia's former position in Manchuria. Already, according to The Times correspondent in Peking, Outer Mongolia, a country about as large as England, France and Germany combined, has been conquered by Bolshevik armies and propaganda.

The Bolsheviks have, of course, the enthusiastic sympathy of the younger Chinese students. If they can weather their present troubles, they have a good chance of being accepted by all vigorous progressive people in Asia as the liberators of Asia from the tyranny of the Great Powers. As they were not invited to Washington, they are not a party to any of the agreements reached there, and it may turn out that they will upset impartially the ambitions of Japan, Great Britain and America.[21] For America, no less than other Powers, has ambitions, though they are economic rather than territorial. If America is victorious in the Far East, China will be Americanized, and though the shell of political freedom may remain, there will be an economic and cultural bondage beneath it. Russia is not strong enough to dominate in this way, but may become strong enough to secure some real freedom for China. This, however, is as yet no more than a possibility. It is worth remembering, because everybody chooses to forget it, and because, while Russia is treated as a pariah, no settlement of the Far East can be stable. But what part Russia is going to play in the affairs of China it is as yet impossible to say.

## NOTES

1   On this subject George Gleason, *What Shall I Think of Japan?* pp. 174–5, says: "This paragraph concerns the iron and steel mills at the city of Han-yang, which, with Wuchang and Hangkow, form the Upper Yangtze commer-cial centre with a population of 1,500,000 people. The Hanyeping Company owns a large part of the Tayeh iron mines, eighty miles east of Hangkow, with which there are water and rail connections. The ore is 67 per cent iron, fills the whole of a series of hills 500 feet high, and is sufficient to turn out 1,000,000 tons a year for 700 years. [Probably an overstatement.] Coal for the furnaces is obtained from Pinghsiang, 200 miles distant by water, where in 1913 five thousand miners dug 690,000 tons. Japanese have estimated that the vein is capable of producing yearly a million tons for at least five centuries. . . .

"Thus did Japan attempt to enter and control a vital spot in the heart of China which for many years Great Britain has regarded as her special trade domain."

Mr. Gleason is an American, not an Englishman. The best account of this matter is given by Mr. Coleman, *The Far East Unveiled,* chaps. x.-xiv. See below, pp. 232–3.

2   See letter from Mr. Eugene Chen, *Japan Weekly Chronicle,* October 20, 1921.

3   The Notes embodying this agreement are quoted in Pooley, *Japan's Foreign Policies,* Allen & Unwin, 1920, pp. 141–2.

4   On this subject, Baron Hayashi, now Japanese Ambassador to the United Kingdom, said to Mr. Coleman: "When Viscount Kato sent China a Note con-taining five groups, however, and then sent to England what purported to be a copy of his Note to China, and that copy only contained four of the groups and omitted the fifth altogether, which was directly a breach of the agreement contained in the Anglo-Japanese Alliance, he did something which I can no more explain than you can. Outside of the question of probity involved, his action was unbelievably foolish" *(The Far East Unveiled,* p. 73).

5   The demands in their original and revised forms, with the negotiations con-cerning them, are printed in Appendix B of *Democracy and the Eastern Ques-tion,* by Thomas F. Millard, Allen & Unwin, 1919.

6   The texts concerned in the various stages of the Shantung question are printed in S. G. Cheng's *Modern China,* Appendix ii, iii and ix. For text of Ishii-Lansing Agreement, see Gleason, op. cit. pp. 214–6.

7   Three books, all by Americans, give the secret and official history of this mat-ter. They are: *An American Diplomat in China,* by Paul S. Reinsch, Doubleday, Page & Co., 1922; *Democracy and the Eastern Question,* by Thomas F. Millard, Allen & Unwin, 1919; and *China, Captive or Free?* by the Rev. Gilbert Reid, A.M., D.D., Director of International Institute of China, Allen & Unwin, 1922.

8   Millard, p. 99.

9   See Pooley, *Japan's Foreign Policies,* pp. 23 ff; Coleman, *The Far East Unveiled,* chap. v., and Millard, chap. iii.

10  Millard, pp. 64–66.

11  Reid, op. cit. pp. 114–5; Cheng, op. cit. pp. 343–6.

12  See Appendix III of Cheng's *Modern China,* which contains this note (p. 346) as well as the other "documents relative to the negotiations between Japan and the Allied Powers as to the disposal of the German rights in respect of Shantung Province, and the South Sea Islands north of the Equator."

13  The story of the steps leading up to China's declaration of war is admirably told in Reid, op. cit. pp. 88–109.

14  Part of the letter is quoted by Dr. Reid, p. 108.

15  Reid, op. cit. p. 161. Chap. vii of this book, "Commercial Rivalries as affecting China," should be read by anyone who still thinks that the Allies stood for honesty or mercy or anything except money-grubbing.

16  Appendix C, pp. 421–4.

17  A list of these loans is given by Hollington K. Tong in an article on "China's Finances in 1918" in *China in 1918,* published early in 1919 by the Peking leader, pp. 61–2. The list and some of the comments appear also in Putnam Weale's *The Truth about China and Japan.*

18  Mr. Lansing's book, in so far as it deals with Japanese questions, is severely criticized from a Japanese point of view in Dr. Y. Soyeda's pamphlet "Shantung Question and Japanese Case," League of Nations Association of Japan, June 1921. I do not think Dr. Soyeda's arguments are likely to appeal to anyone who is not Japanese.

19  See the clauses concerning Shantung, in full, in Cheng's *Modern China,* Clarendon Press, pp. 360–1.

20  This agitation is well described in Mr. M. T. Z. Tyau's *China Awakened* (Macmillan, 1922) chap. ix., "The Student Movement."

21  "Soviet Russia has addressed to the Powers a protest against the discussion at the Washington Conference of the East China Railway, a question exclusively affecting China and Russia, and declares that it reserves for itself full liberty of action in order to compel due deference to the rights of the Russian labouring masses and to make demands consistent with those rights" *(Daily Herald,* December 22, 1921). This is the new-style imperialism. It was not the "Russian labouring masses," but the Chinese coolies, who built the railway. What Russia contributed was capital, but one is surprised to find the Bolsheviks considering that this confers rights upon themselves as heirs of the capitalists.

# 9

## THE WASHINGTON CONFERENCE

The Washington Conference, and the simultaneous conference, at Washington, between the Chinese and Japanese, have somewhat modified the Far Eastern situation. The general aspects of the new situation will be dealt with in the next chapter; for the present it is the actual decisions arrived at in Washington that concern us, as well as their effect upon the Japanese position in Siberia.

In the first place, the Anglo-Japanese Alliance has apparently been brought to an end, as a result of the conclusion of the Four Power Pact between America, Great Britain, France and Japan. Within this general alliance of the exploiting Powers, there is a subordinate grouping of America and Great Britain against France and Japan, the former standing for international capitalism, the latter for national capitalism. The situation is not yet plain, because England and America disagree as regards Russia, and because America is not yet prepared to take part in the reconstruction of Europe; but in the Far East, at any rate, we seem to have decided to seek the friendship of America rather than of Japan. It may perhaps be hoped that this will make our Chinese policy more liberal than it has been. We have announced the restoration of Wei-hai-wei—a piece of generosity which would have been more impressive but for two facts: first, that Wei-hai-wei is completely useless to us, and secondly, that the lease had only two more years to run. By the terms of the lease, in fact, it should have been restored as soon as Russia lost Port Arthur, however many years it still had to run at that date.

One very important result of the Washington Conference is the agreement not to fortify islands in the Pacific, with certain specified exceptions. This agreement, if it is adhered to, will make war between America and Japan very difficult, unless we were allied with America. Without a naval base somewhere near Japan, America could hardly bring naval force to bear on the Japanese Navy. It had been the intention of the Navy Department to fortify Guam with a view to turning it into a first-class naval base. The fact that America has been willing to forgo this intention must be taken as evidence of a genuine desire to preserve the peace with Japan.

Various small concessions were made to China. There is to be a revision of the Customs Schedule to bring it to an effective five per cent. The foreign Post Offices are to be abolished, though the Japanese have insisted that a certain number of Japanese should be employed in the Chinese Post Office. They had the effrontery to pretend that they desired this for the sake of the efficiency of the postal service, though the Chinese post is excellent and the Japanese is notoriously one of the worst in the world. The chief use to which the Japanese have put their postal service in China has been the importation of morphia, as they have not allowed the Chinese Customs authorities to examine parcels sent through their Post Office. The development of the Japanese importation of morphia into China, as well as the growth of the poppy in Manchuria, where they have control, has been a very sinister feature of their penetration of China.[1]

Of course the Open Door, equality of opportunity, the independence and integrity of China, etc. etc., were reaffirmed at Washington; but these are mere empty phrases devoid of meaning.

From the Chinese point of view, the chief achievement at Washington was the Shantung Treaty. Ever since the expulsion by the Germans at the end of 1914, the Japanese had held Kiaochow Bay, which includes the port of Tsingtau; they had stationed troops along the whole extent of the Shantung Railway; and by the treaty following the Twenty-one Demands, they had preferential treatment as regards all industrial undertakings in Shantung. The railway belonged to them by right of conquest, and through it they acquired control of the whole province. When an excuse was needed for increasing the garrison, they supplied arms to brigands, and claimed that their intervention was necessary to suppress the resulting disorder. This state of affairs was legalized by the Treaty of Versailles, to which, however, America and China were not parties. The Washington Conference, therefore, supplied an opportunity of raising the question afresh.

At first, however, it seemed as if the Japanese would have things all their own way. The Chinese wished to raise the question before the Conference, while the Japanese wished to settle it in direct negotiation with China. This point was important, because, ever since the Lansing-Ishii agreement, the Japanese have tried to get the Powers to recognize, in practice if not in theory, an informal Japanese Protectorate over China, as a first step towards which it was necessary to establish the principle that the Japanese should not be interfered with in their diplomatic dealings with China. The Conference agreed to the Japanese proposal that the Shantung question should not come before the Conference, but should be dealt with in direct negotiations between the Japanese and Chinese. The Japanese victory on this point, however, was not complete, because it was arranged that, in the event of a deadlock, Mr. Hughes and Sir Arthur Balfour should mediate. A deadlock, of course, soon occurred, and it then appeared that the British were no longer prepared to back up the Japanese whole-heartedly, as in the old days. The American Administration, for the sake of peace, showed some disposition to urge the Chinese to give way. But American opinion was roused on the Shantung question, and it appeared that, unless a solution more or less satisfactory to China was reached, the Senate would probably refuse to ratify the various treaties which embodied the work of the Conference. Therefore, at the last moment, the Americans strongly urged Japan to give way, and we took the same line, though perhaps less strongly. The result was the conclusion of the Shantung Treaty between China and Japan.

By this Treaty, the Chinese recover everything in Shantung, except the private property of Japanese subjects, and certain restrictions as regards the railway. The railway was the great difficulty in the negotiations, since, so long as the Japanese could control that, they would have the province at their mercy. The Chinese offered to buy back the railway at once, having raised about half the money as a result of a patriotic movement among their merchants. This, however, the Japanese refused to agree to. What was finally done was that the Chinese were compelled to borrow the money from the Japanese Government to be repaid in fifteen years, with an option of repayment in five years. The railway was valued at 53,400,000 gold marks, plus the costs involved in repairs or improvements incurred by Japan, less deterioration; and it was to be handed over to China within nine months of the signature of the treaty. Until the purchase price, borrowed from Japan, is repaid, the Japanese retain a certain degree of control over the railway: a Japanese traffic manager is to be appointed, and two accountants, one Chinese and the other Japanese, under the control of a Chinese President.

It is clear that, on paper, this gives the Chinese everything five years hence. Whether things will work out so depends upon whether, five years hence, any Power is prepared to force Japan to keep her word. As both Mr. Hughes and Sir Arthur Balfour strongly urged the Chinese to agree to this compromise, it must be assumed that America and Great Britain have some responsibility for seeing that it is properly carried out. In that case, we may perhaps expect that in the end China will acquire complete control of the Shantung railway.

On the whole, it must be said that China did better at Washington than might have been expected. As regards the larger aspects of the new international situation arising out of the Conference, I shall deal with them in the next chapter. But in our present connection it is necessary to consider certain Far Eastern questions *not* discussed at Washington, since the mere fact that they were not discussed gave them a new form.

The question of Manchuria and Inner Mongolia was not raised at Washington. It may therefore be assumed that Japan's position there is secure until such time as the Chinese, or the Russians, or both together, are strong enough to challenge it. America, at any rate, will not raise the question unless friction occurs on some other issue. (See Appendix.)

The Siberian question also was not settled. Therefore Japan's ambitions in Vladivostok and the Maritime Provinces will presumably remain unchecked except in so far as the Russians unaided are able to check them. There is a chronic state of semi-war between the Japanese and the Far Eastern Republic, and there seems no reason why it should end in any near future. The Japanese from time to time announce that they have decided to withdraw, but they simultaneously send fresh troops. A conference between them and the Chita Government has been taking place at Dairen, and from time to time announcements have appeared to the effect that an agreement has been reached or was about to be reached. But on April 16th (1922) the Japanese broke up the Conference. *The Times* of April 27th contains both the Japanese and the Russian official accounts of this break up. The Japanese statement is given in *The Times* as follows:—

The Japanese Embassy communicates the text of a statement given out on April 20th by the Japanese Foreign Office on the Dairen Conference.

It begins by recalling that in response to the repeatedly expressed desire of the Chita Government, the Japanese Government decided to enter into negotiations. The first meeting took place on August 26th last year.

The Japanese demands included the non-enforcement of communistic principles in the Republic against Japanese, the prohibition of Bolshevist propaganda, the abolition of menacing military establishments, the adoption of the principle of the open door in Siberia, and the removal of industrial restrictions on foreigners. Desiring speedily to conclude an agreement, so that the withdrawal of troops might be carried out as soon as possible, Japan met the wishes of Chita as far as practicable. Though, from the outset, Chita pressed for a speedy settlement of the Nicolaievsk affair, Japan eventually agreed to take up the Nicolaievsk affair immediately after the conclusion of the basis agreement. She further assured Chita that in settling the affair Japan had no intention of violating the sovereignty and territorial integrity of Russia, and that the troops would be speedily withdrawn from Saghalin after the settlement of the affair, and that Chita's wishes in regard to the transfer of property now in the custody of the Japanese authorities would be met.

The 11th Division of the troops in Siberia was originally to be relieved during April, but if the Dairen Conference had progressed satisfactorily, the troops, instead of being relieved, would have been sent home. Japan therefore intimated to Chita that should the basis agreement be concluded within a reasonable period these troops would be immediately withdrawn, and proposed the signature of the agreement by the middle of April, so that the preparations for the relief of the said division might be dispensed with. Thereupon Chita not only proposed the immediate despatch of Chita troops to Vladivostok without waiting for the withdrawal of the Japanese troops, but urged that Japan should fix a time-limit for the complete withdrawal of all her troops.

Japan informed Chita that the withdrawal would be carried out within a short period after the conclusion of the detailed arrangements, giving a definite period as desired, and at the same time she proposed the signing of the agreement drawn up by Japan.

Whereas Japan thus throughout the negotiations maintained a sincere and conciliatory attitude, the Chita delegates entirely ignored the spirit in which she offered concessions and brought up one demand after another, thereby trying to gain time. Not only did they refuse to entertain the Japanese proposals, but declared that they would drop the negotiations and return to Chita immediately. The only conclusion from this attitude of the Chita Government is that they lacked a sincere effort to bring the negotiations to fruition, and the Japanese Government instructed its delegates to quit Dairen.

The Russian official account is given by *The Times* immediately below the above. It is as follows:—

On April 16th the Japanese broke up the Dairen Conference with the Far Eastern Republic. The Far Eastern Delegation left Dairen. Agreement was reached between the Japanese and Russian Delegations on March 30th on all points of the general treaty, but when the question of military evacuation was reached the Japanese Delegation proposed a formula permitting continued Japanese intervention.

Between March 30th and April 15th the Japanese dragged on the negotiations *re* military convention, reproaching the Far Eastern delegates for mistrusting the Japanese Government. The Russian Delegation declared that the general treaty would be signed only upon obtaining precise written guarantees of Japanese military evacuation.

On April 15th the Japanese Delegation presented an ultimatum demanding a reply from the Far Eastern representatives in half an hour as to whether they were willing to sign a general agreement with new Japanese conditions forbidding an increase in the Far Eastern Navy and retaining a Japanese military mission on Far Eastern territory. *Re* evacuation, the Japanese presented a Note promising evacuation if "not prevented by unforeseen circumstances." The Russian Delegation rejected this ultimatum. On April 16th the Japanese declared the Dairen Conference broken up. The Japanese delegates left for Tokyo, and Japanese troops remain in the zone established by the agreement of March 29th.

Readers will believe one or other of these official statements according to their prejudices, while those who wish to think themselves impartial will assume that the truth lies somewhere between the two. For my part, I believe the Russian statement. But even from the Japanese communiqué it is evident that what wrecked the Conference was Japanese unwillingness to evacuate Vladivostok and the Maritime Province; all that they were willing to give was a vague promise to evacuate some day, which would have had no more value than Mr. Gladstone's promise to evacuate Egypt.

It will be observed that the Conference went well for Chita until the Senate had ratified the Washington treaties. After that, the Japanese felt that they had a free hand in all Far Eastern matters not dealt with at Washington. The practical effect of the Washington decisions will naturally be to make the Japanese seek compensation, at the expense of the Far Eastern Republic, for what they have had to surrender in China. This result was to be expected, and was presumably foreseen by the assembled peacemakers.[2]

It will be seen that the Japanese policy involves hostility to Russia. This is no doubt one reason for the friendship between Japan and France. Another reason is that both are the champions of nationalistic capitalism, as against the international capitalism aimed at by Messrs. Morgan and Mr. Lloyd George, because France and Japan look to their armaments as the chief source of their income, while England and America look rather to their commerce and industry. It would be interesting to compute how much coal and iron France and Japan have acquired in recent years by means of their armies. England and America already possessed coal and iron; hence their different policy. An uninvited delegation from the Far Eastern Republic at Washington produced documents tending to show that France and Japan came there as secret allies. Although the authenticity of the documents was denied, most people, apparently, believed them to be genuine. In any case, it is to be expected that France and Japan will stand together, now that the Anglo-Japanese Alliance has come to an end and the Anglo-French Entente has become anything but cordial. Thus it is to be feared that Washington and Genoa have sown the seeds of future wars—unless, by some miracle, the "civilized" nations should grow weary of suicide.

## NOTES

1   See *e.g.* chap. viii. of Millard's *Democracy and the Eastern Question.*
2   I ought perhaps to confess that I have a bias in favour of the Far Eastern Republic, owing to my friendship for their diplomatic mission which was in Peking while I was there. I never met a more high-minded set of men in any country. And although they were communists, and knew the views that I had expressed on Russia, they showed me great kindness. I do not think, however, that these courtesies have affected my view of the dispute between Chita and Tokyo.

# 10

## PRESENT FORCES AND TENDENCIES IN THE FAR EAST

The Far Eastern situation is so complex that it is very difficult to guess what will be the ultimate outcome of the Washington Conference, and still more difficult to know what outcome we ought to desire. I will endeavour to set forth the various factors each in turn, not simplifying the issues, but rather aiming at producing a certain hesitancy which I regard as desirable in dealing with China. I shall consider successively the interests and desires of America, Japan, Russia and China, with an attempt, in each case, to gauge what parts of these various interests and desires are compatible with the welfare of mankind as a whole.[1]

I begin with America, as the leading spirit in the Conference and the dominant Power in the world. American public opinion is in favour of peace, and at the same time profoundly persuaded that America is wise and virtuous while all other Powers are foolish and wicked. The pessimistic half of this opinion I do not desire to dispute, but the optimistic half is more open to question. Apart from peace, American public opinion believes in commerce and industry, Protestant morality, athletics, hygiene, and hypocrisy, which may be taken as the main ingredients of American and English Kultur. Every American I met in the Far East, with one exception, was a missionary for American Kultur, whether nominally connected with Christian Missions or not. I ought to explain that when I speak of hypocrisy I do not mean the conscious hypocrisy practised by Japanese diplomats in their dealings with Western Powers, but that deeper, unconscious kind which forms the chief strength of the Anglo-Saxons. Everybody knows Labouchere's comment on Mr. Gladstone, that like other politicians he always had a card up his sleeve, but, unlike the others, he thought the Lord had put it there. This attitude, which has been characteristic of England, has been somewhat chastened among ourselves by the satire of men like Bernard Shaw; but in America it is still just as prevalent and self-confident as it was with us fifty years ago. There is much justification for such an attitude. Gladstonian England was more of a moral force than the England of the present day; and America is more of a moral force at this moment than any other Power (except Russia). But the development from Gladstone's moral fervour to the cynical imperialism of his successors is one which we can now see to be inevitable; and a similar development is bound to take place in the United States. Therefore, when we wish to estimate the desirability of extending the influence of the United States, we have to take account of this almost certain future loss of idealism.

Nor is idealism in itself always an unmixed blessing to its victims. It is apt to be incompatible with tolerance, with the practice of live-and-let-live, which alone can make the world endurable for its less pugnacious and energetic inhabitants. It is difficult for art or the contemplative outlook to exist in an atmosphere of bustling practical philanthropy, as difficult as it would be to write a book in the middle of a spring cleaning. The ideals which inspire a spring-cleaning are useful and valuable in their place, but when they are not enriched by any others they are apt to produce a rather bleak and uncomfortable sort of world.

All this may seem, at first sight, somewhat remote from the Washington Conference, but it is essential if we are to take a just view of the friction between America and Japan. I wish to admit at once that, hitherto, America has been the best friend of China, and Japan the worst enemy. It is also true that America is doing more than any other Power to promote peace in the world, while Japan would probably favour war if there were a good prospect of victory. On these grounds, I am glad to see our Government making friends with America and abandoning the militaristic Anglo-Japanese Alliance. But I do not wish this to be done in a spirit of hostility to Japan, or in a blind reliance upon the future good intentions of America. I shall therefore try to state Japan's case, although, for the present, I think it weaker than America's.

It should be observed, in the first place, that the present American policy, both in regard to China and in regard to naval armaments, while clearly good for the world, is quite as clearly in line with American interests. To take the naval question first: America, with a navy equal to our own, will be quite strong enough to make our Admiralty understand that it is out of the question to go to war with America, so that America will have as much control of the seas as there is any point in having.[2] The Americans are adamant about the Japanese Navy, but very pliant about French submarines, which only threaten us. Control of the seas being secured, limitation of naval armaments merely decreases the cost, and is an equal gain to all parties, involving no sacrifice of American interests. To take next the question of China: American ambitions in China are economic, and require only that the whole country should be open to the commerce and industry of the United States. The policy of spheres of influence is obviously less advantageous, to so rich and economically strong a country as America, than the policy of the universal Open Door. We cannot therefore regard America's liberal policy as regards China and naval armaments as any reason for expecting a liberal policy when it goes against self-interest.

In fact, there is evidence that when American interests or prejudices are involved liberal and humanitarian principles have no weight whatever. I will cite two instances: Panama tolls, and Russian trade.

In the matter of the Panama canal, America is bound by treaty not to discriminate against our shipping; nevertheless a Bill has been passed by a two-thirds majority of the House of Representatives, making a discrimination in favour of American shipping. Even if the President ultimately vetoes it, its present position shows that at least two-thirds of the House of Representatives share Bethmann-Hollweg's view of treaty obligations. And as for trade with Russia, England led the way, while American hostility to the Bolsheviks remained implacable, and to this day Gompers, in the name of American labour, thunders against "shaking hands with murder." It cannot therefore be said that America is *always* honourable or humanitarian or liberal. The evidence is that America adopts these virtues when they suit national or rather financial interests, but fails to perceive their applicability in other cases.

I could of course have given many other instances, but I content myself with one, because it especially concerns China. I quote from an American weekly, The *Freeman* (November 23, 1921, p. 244):—

On November 1st, the Chinese Government failed to meet an obligation of $5,500,000, due and payable to a large banking-house in Chicago. The State Department had facilitated the negotiation of this loan in the first instance; and now, in fulfilment of the promise of Governmental support in an emergency, an official cablegram was launched upon Peking, with intimations that continued defalcation might have a most serious effect upon the financial and political rating of the Chinese Republic. In the meantime, the American bankers of the new international consortium had offered to advance to the Chinese Government an amount which would cover the loan in default, together with other obligations already in arrears, and still others which will fall due on December 1st; and this proposal had also received the full and energetic support of the Department of State. That is to say, American financiers and politicians were at one and the same time the heroes and villains of the piece; having co-operated in the creation of a dangerous situation, they came forward handsomely in the hour of trial with an offer to save China from themselves as it were, if the Chinese

Government would only enter into relations with the consortium, and thus prepare the way for the eventual establishment of an American financial protectorate.

It should be added that the Peking Government, after repeated negotiations, had decided not to accept loans from the consortium on the terms on which they were offered. In my opinion, there were very adequate grounds for this decision. As the same article in the *Freeman* concludes:—

> If this plan is put through, it will make the bankers of the consortium the virtual owners of China; and among these bankers, those of the United States are the only ones who are prepared to take full advantage of the situation.

There is some reason to think that, at the beginning of the Washington Conference, an attempt was made by the consortium banks, with the connivance of the British but not of the American Government, to establish, by means of the Conference, some measure of international control over China. In the *Japan Weekly Chronicle* for November 17, 1921 (p. 725), in a telegram headed "International Control of China," I find it reported that America is thought to be seeking to establish international control, and that Mr. Wellington Koo told the *Philadelphia Public Ledger*: "We suspect the motives which led to the suggestion and we thoroughly doubt its feasibility. China will bitterly oppose any Conference plan to offer China international aid." He adds: "International control will not do. China must be given time and opportunity to find herself. The world should not misinterpret or exaggerate the meaning of the convulsion which China is now passing through." These are wise words, with which every true friend of China must agree. In the same issue of the *Japan Weekly Chronicle*—which, by the way, I consider the best weekly paper in the world—I find the following (p. 728):—

> Mr. Lennox Simpson [Putnam Weale] is quoted as saying: "The international bankers have a scheme for the international control of China.

> Mr. Lamont, representing the consortium, offered a sixteen-million-dollar loan to China, which the Chinese Government refused to accept because Mr. Lamont insisted that the Hukuang bonds, German issue, which had been acquired by the Morgan Company, should be paid out of it." Mr. Lamont, on hearing this charge, made an emphatic denial, saying: "Simpson's statement is unqualifiedly false. When this man Simpson talks about resisting the control of the international banks he is fantastic. We don't want control. We are anxious that the Conference result in such a solution as will furnish full opportunity to China to fulfil her own destiny."

Sagacious people will be inclined to conclude that so much anger must be due to being touched on the raw, and that Mr. Lamont, if he had had nothing to conceal, would not have spoken of a distinguished writer and one of China's best friends as "this man Simpson."

I do not pretend that the evidence against the consortium is conclusive, and I have not space here to set it all forth. But to any European radical Mr. Lamont's statement that the consortium does not want control reads like a contradiction in terms. Those who wish to lend to a Government which is on the verge of bankruptcy, must aim at control, for, even if there were not the incident of the Chicago Bank, it would be impossible to believe that Messrs. Morgan are so purely philanthropic as not to care whether they get any interest on their money or not, although emissaries of the consortium in China have spoken as though this were the case, thereby greatly increasing the suspicions of the Chinese.

In the *New Republic* for November 30, 1921, there is an article by Mr. Brailsford entitled "A New Technique of Peace," which I fear is prophetic even if not wholly applicable at the moment when it was written. I expect to see, if the Americans are successful in the Far East, China compelled to be orderly so as to afford a field for foreign commerce and industry; a government which the West will consider good substituted for the present go-as-you-please anarchy; a gradually increasing flow of wealth from China to the investing countries, the chief of which is America; the development of a sweated proletariat;

the spread of Christianity; the substitution of the American civilization for the Chinese; the destruction of traditional beauty, except for
such *objets d'art* as millionaires may think it worth while to buy; the
gradual awakening of China to her exploitation by the foreigner; and
one day, fifty or a hundred years hence, the massacre of every white
man throughout the Celestial Empire at a signal from some vast secret
society. All this is probably inevitable, human nature being what it is. It
will be done in order that rich men may grow richer, but we shall be
told that it is done in order that China may have "good" government.
The definition of the word "good" is difficult, but the definition of
"good government" is as easy as A.B.C.: it is government that yields fat
dividends to capitalists.

The Chinese are gentle, urbane, seeking only justice and freedom.
They have a civilization superior to ours in all that makes for human
happiness. They have a vigorous movement of young reformers, who,
if they are allowed a little time, will revivify China and produce something immeasurably better than the worn-out grinding mechanism that
we call civilization. When Young China has done its work, Americans
will be able to make money by trading with China, without destroying the soul of the country. China needs a period of anarchy in order
to work out her salvation; all great nations need such a period, from
time to time. When America went through such a period, in 1861–5,
England thought of intervening to insist on "good government," but
fortunately abstained. Now-a-days, in China, all the Powers want to intervene. Americans recognize this in the case of the wicked Old World,
but are smitten with blindness when it comes to their own consortium.
All I ask of them is that they should admit that they are as other men,
and cease to thank God that they are not as this publican.

So much by way of criticism by America; we come now to the defence of Japan.

Japan's relations with the Powers are not of her own seeking; all that
Japan asked of the world was to be let alone. This, however, did not suit
the white nations, among whom America led the way. It was a United
States squadron under Commodore Perry that first made Japan aware
of Western aggressiveness. Very soon it became evident that there were

only two ways of dealing with the white man, either to submit to him, or to fight him with his own weapons. Japan adopted the latter course, and developed a modern army trained by the Germans, a modern navy modelled on the British, modern machinery derived from America, and modern morals copied from the whole lot. Everybody except the British was horrified, and called the Japanese "yellow monkeys." However, they began to be respected when they defeated Russia, and after they had captured Tsing-tao and half-enslaved China they were admitted to equality with the other Great Powers at Versailles. The consideration shown to them by the West is due to their armaments alone; none of their other good qualities would have saved them from being regarded as "niggers."

People who have never been outside Europe can hardly imagine the intensity of the colour prejudice that white men develop when brought into contact with any different pigmentation. I have seen Chinese of the highest education, men as cultured as (say) Dean Inge, treated by greasy white men as if they were dirt, in a way in which, at home, no Duke would venture to treat a crossing-sweeper. The Japanese are not treated in this way, because they have a powerful army and navy. The fact that white men, as individuals, no longer dare to bully individual Japanese, is important as a beginning of better relations towards the coloured races in general. If the Japanese, by defeat in war, are prevented from retaining the status of a Great Power, the coloured races in general will suffer, and the tottering insolence of the white man will be re-established. Also the world will have lost the last chance of the survival of civilizations of a different type from that of the industrial West.

The civilization of Japan, in its material aspect, is similar to that of the West, though industrialism, as yet, is not very developed. But in its mental aspect it is utterly unlike the West, particularly the Anglo-Saxon West. Worship of the Mikado, as an actually divine being, is successfully taught in every village school, and provides the popular support for nationalism. The nationalistic aims of Japan are not merely economic; they are also dynastic and territorial in a mediaeval way. The morality of the Japanese is not utilitarian, but intensely idealistic.

Filial piety is the basis, and includes patriotism, because the Mikado is the father of his people. The Japanese outlook has the same kind of superstitious absence of realism that one finds in thirteenth-century theories as to the relations of the Emperor and the Pope. But in Europe the Emperor and the Pope were different people, and their quarrels promoted freedom of thought; in Japan, since 1868, they are combined in one sacred person, and there are no internal conflicts to produce doubt.

Japan, unlike China, is a religious country. The Chinese doubt a proposition until it is proved to be true; the Japanese believe it until it is proved to be false. I do not know of any evidence against the view that the Mikado is divine. Japanese religion is essentially nationalistic, like that of the Jews in the Old Testament. Shinto, the State religion, has been in the main invented since 1868,[3] and propagated by education in schools. (There was of course an old Shinto religion, but most of what constitutes modern Shintoism is new.) It is not a religion which aims at being universal, like Buddhism, Christianity, and Islam; it is a tribal religion, only intended to appeal to the Japanese. Buddhism subsists side by side with it, and is believed by the same people. It is customary to adopt Shinto rites for marriages and Buddhist rites for funerals, because Buddhism is considered more suitable for mournful occasions. Although Buddhism is a universal religion, its Japanese form is intensely national,[4] like the Church of England. Many of its priests marry, and in some temples the priesthood is hereditary. Its dignitaries remind one vividly of English Archdeacons.

The Japanese, even when they adopt industrial methods, do not lose their sense of beauty. One hears complaints that their goods are shoddy, but they have a remarkable power of adapting artistic taste to industrialism. If Japan were rich it might produce cities as beautiful as Venice, by methods as modern as those of New York. Industrialism has hitherto brought with it elsewhere a rising tide of ugliness, and any nation which can show us how to make this tide recede deserves our gratitude.

The Japanese are earnest, passionate, strong-willed, amazingly hard working, and capable of boundless sacrifice to an ideal. Most of them have the correlative defects: lack of humour, cruelty, intolerance, and incapacity for free thought. But these defects are by no means universal; one meets among them a certain number of men and women of quite extraordinary excellence. And there is in their civilization as a whole a degree of vigour and determination which commands the highest respect.

The growth of industrialism in Japan has brought with it the growth of Socialism and the Labour movement.[5] In China, the intellectuals are often theoretical Socialists, but in the absence of Labour organizations there is as yet little room for more than theory. In Japan, Trade Unionism has made considerable advances, and every variety of socialist and anarchist opinion is vigorously represented. In time, if Japan becomes increasingly industrial, Socialism may become a political force; as yet, I do not think it is. Japanese Socialists resemble those of other countries, in that they do not share the national superstitions. They are much persecuted by the Government, but not so much as Socialists in America—so at least I am informed by an American who is in a position to judge.

The real power is still in the hands of certain aristocratic families. By the constitution, the Ministers of War and Marine are directly responsible to the Mikado, not to the Diet or the Prime Minister. They therefore can and do persist in policies which are disliked by the Foreign Office. For example, if the Foreign Office were to promise the evacuation of Vladivostok, the War Office might nevertheless decide to keep the soldiers there, and there would be no constitutional remedy. Some part, at least, of what appears as Japanese bad faith is explicable in this way. There is of course a party which wishes to establish real Parliamentary government, but it is not likely to come into power unless the existing régime suffers some severe diplomatic humiliation. If the Washington Conference had compelled the evacuation of not only Shantung but also Vladivostok by diplomatic pressure, the effect on the internal government of Japan would probably have been excellent.

The Japanese are firmly persuaded that they have no friends, and that the Americans are their implacable foes. One gathers that the

Government regards war with America as unavoidable in the long run. The argument would be that the economic imperialism of the United States will not tolerate the industrial development of a formidable rival in the Pacific, and that sooner or later the Japanese will be presented with the alternative of dying by starvation or on the battlefield. Then Bushido will come into play, and will lead to choice of the battlefield in preference to starvation. Admiral Sato[6] (the Japanese Bernhardi, as he is called) maintains that absence of Bushido in the Americans will lead to their defeat, and that their money-grubbing souls will be incapable of enduring the hardships and privations of a long war. This, of course, is romantic nonsense. Bushido is no use in modern war, and the Americans are quite as courageous and obstinate as the Japanese. A war might last ten years, but it would certainly end in the defeat of Japan.

One is constantly reminded of the situation between England and Germany in the years before 1914. The Germans wanted to acquire a colonial empire by means similar to those which we had employed; so do the Japanese. We considered such methods wicked when employed by foreigners; so do the Americans. The Germans developed their industries and roused our hostility by competition; the Japanese are similarly competing with America in Far Eastern markets. The Germans felt themselves encircled by our alliances, which we regarded as purely defensive; the Japanese, similarly, found themselves isolated at Washington (except for French sympathy) since the superior diplomatic skill of the Americans has brought us over to their side. The Germans at last, impelled by terrors largely of their own creation, challenged the whole world, and fell; it is very much to be feared that Japan may do likewise. The pros and cons are so familiar in the case of Germany that I need not elaborate them further, since the whole argument can be transferred bodily to the case of Japan. There is, however, this difference, that, while Germany aimed at hegemony of the whole world, the Japanese only aim at hegemony in Eastern Asia.

The conflict between America and Japan is superficially economic, but, as often happens, the economic rivalry is really a cloak for deeper passions. Japan still believes in the divine right of kings; America believes in the divine right of commerce. I have sometimes tried to persuade Americans that there may be nations which will not gain by an extension of their foreign commerce, but I have always found the attempt futile. The Americans believe also that their religion and morality and culture are far superior to those of the Far East. I regard this as a delusion, though one shared by almost all Europeans. The Japanese, profoundly and with all the strength of their being, long to preserve their own culture and to avoid becoming like Europeans or Americans; and in this I think we ought to sympathize with them. The colour prejudice is even more intense among Americans than among Europeans; the Japanese are determined to prove that the yellow man may be the equal of the white man. In this, also, justice and humanity are on the side of Japan. Thus on the deeper issues, which underlie the economic and diplomatic conflict, my feelings go with the Japanese rather than with the Americans.

Unfortunately, the Japanese are always putting themselves in the wrong through impatience and contempt. They ought to have claimed for China the same consideration that they have extorted towards themselves; then they could have become, what they constantly profess to be, the champions of Asia against Europe. The Chinese are prone to gratitude, and would have helped Japan loyally if Japan had been a true friend to them. But the Japanese despise the Chinese more than the Europeans do; they do not want to destroy the belief in Eastern inferiority, but only to be regarded as themselves belonging to the West. They have therefore behaved so as to cause a well-deserved hatred of them in China. And this same behaviour has made the best Americans as hostile to them as the worst. If America had had none but base reasons for hostility to them, they would have found many champions in the United States; as it is, they have practically none. It is not yet too late; it is still possible for them to win the affection of China and the respect of the best Americans. To achieve this, they would have to change their Chinese policy and adopt a more democratic constitution; but if they do not achieve it, they will fall as Germany fell. And their fall will be a great misfortune for mankind.

A war between America and Japan would be a very terrible thing in itself, and a still more terrible thing in its consequences. It would destroy Japanese civilization, ensure the subjugation of China to Western culture, and launch America upon a career of world-wide militaristic imperialism. It is therefore, at all costs, to be avoided. If it is to be avoided, Japan must become more liberal; and Japan will only become more liberal if the present régime is discredited by failure. Therefore, in the interests of Japan no less than in the interests of China, it would be well if Japan were forced, by the joint diplomatic pressure of England and America, to disgorge, not only Shantung, but also all of Manchuria except Port Arthur and its immediate neighbourhood. (I make this exception because I think nothing short of actual war would lead the Japanese to abandon Port Arthur.) Our Alliance with Japan, since the end of the Russo-Japanese war, has been an encouragement to Japan in all that she has done amiss. Not that Japan has been worse than we have, but that certain kinds of crime are only permitted to very great Powers, and have been committed by the Japanese at an earlier stage of their career than prudence would warrant. Our Alliance has been a contributory cause of Japan's mistakes, and the ending of the Alliance is a necessary condition of Japanese reform.

We come now to Russia's part in the Chinese problem. There is a tendency in Europe to regard Russia as decrepit, but this is a delusion. True, millions are starving and industry is at a standstill. But that does not mean what it would in a more highly organized country. Russia is still able to steal a march on us in Persia and Afghanistan, and on the Japanese in Outer Mongolia. Russia is still able to organize Bolshevik propaganda in every country in Asia. And a great part of the effectiveness of this propaganda lies in its promise of liberation from Europe. So far, in China proper, it has affected hardly anyone except the younger students, to whom Bolshevism appeals as a method of developing industry without passing through the stage of private capitalism. This appeal will doubtless diminish as the Bolsheviks are more and more forced to revert to capitalism. Moreover, Bolshevism, as it has developed in Russia, is quite peculiarly inapplicable to China, for the following reasons: (1) It requires a strong centralized State, whereas China has a very weak State, and is tending more and more to federalism instead of centralization; (2) Bolshevism requires a very great deal of government, and more control of individual lives by the authorities than has ever been known before, whereas China has developed personal liberty to an extraordinary degree, and is the country of all others where the doctrines of anarchism seem to find successful practical application; (3) Bolshevism dislikes private trading, which is the breath of life to all Chinese except the literati. For these reasons, it is not likely that Bolshevism as a creed will make much progress in China proper. But Bolshevism as a political force is not the same thing as Bolshevism as a creed. The arguments which proved successful with the Ameer of Afghanistan or the nomads of Mongolia were probably different from those employed in discussion with Mr. Lansbury. The Asiatic expansion of Bolshevik influence is not a distinctively Bolshevik phenomenon, but a continuation of traditional Russian policy, carried on by men who are more energetic, more intelligent, and less corrupt than the officials of the Tsar's régime, and who moreover, like the Americans, believe themselves to be engaged in the liberation of mankind, not in mere imperialistic expansion. This belief, of course, adds enormously to the vigour and success of Bolshevik imperialism, and gives an impulse to Asiatic expansion which is not likely to be soon spent, unless there is an actual restoration of the Tsarist regime under some new Kolchak dependent upon alien arms for his throne and his life.

It is therefore not at all unlikely, if the international situation develops in certain ways, that Russia may set to work to regain Manchuria, and to recover that influence over Peking which the control of Manchuria is bound to give to any foreign Power. It would probably be useless to attempt such an enterprise while Japan remains unembarrassed, but it would at once become feasible if Japan were at war with America or with Great Britain. There is therefore nothing improbable in the supposition that Russia may, within the next ten or twenty years, recover the position which she held in relation to China before the Russo-Japanese war. It must be remembered also that the Russians have an instinct for colonization, and have been trekking eastward for centuries. This tendency has been interrupted by the disasters of the last seven years, but is likely to assert itself again before long.

The hegemony of Russia in Asia would not, to my mind, be in any way regrettable. Russia would probably not be strong enough to tyrannize as much as the English, the Americans, or the Japanese would do. Moreover, the Russians are sufficiently Asiatic in outlook and character to be able to enter into relations of equality and mutual understanding with Asiatics, in a way which seems quite impossible for the English-speaking nations. And an Asiatic block, if it could be formed, would be strong for defence and weak for attack, which would make for peace. Therefore, on the whole, such a result, if it came about, would probably be desirable in the interests of mankind as a whole.

What, meanwhile, is China's interest? What would be ideally best for China would be to recover Manchuria and Shantung, and then be let alone. The anarchy in China might take a long time to subside, but in the end some system suited to China would be established. The artificial ending of Chinese anarchy by outside interference means the establishment of some system convenient for foreign trade and industry, but probably quite unfitted to the needs of the Chinese themselves. The English in the seventeenth century, the French in the eighteenth, the Americans in the nineteenth, and the Russians in our own day, have passed through years of anarchy and civil war, which were essential to their development, and could not have been curtailed by outside interference without grave detriment to the final solution. So it is with China. Western political ideas have swept away the old imperial system, but have not yet proved strong enough to put anything stable in its place. The problem of transforming China into a modern country is a difficult one, and foreigners ought to be willing to have some patience while the Chinese attempt its solution. They understand their own country, and we do not. If they are let alone, they will, in the end, find a solution suitable to their character, which we shall certainly not do. A solution slowly reached by themselves may be stable, whereas one prematurely imposed by outside Powers will be artificial and therefore unstable.

There is, however, very little hope that the decisions reached by the Washington Conference will permanently benefit China, and a considerable chance that they may do quite the reverse. In Manchuria the *status quo* is to be maintained, while in Shantung the Japanese have made concessions, the value of which only time can show. The Four Powers—America, Great Britain, France, and Japan—have agreed to exploit China in combination, not competitively. There is a consortium as regards loans, which will have the power of the purse and will therefore be the real Government of China. As the Americans are the only people who have much spare capital, they will control the consortium. As they consider their civilization the finest in the world, they will set to work to turn the Chinese into muscular Christians. As the financiers are the most splendid feature of the American civilization, China must be so governed as to enrich the financiers, who will in return establish colleges and hospitals and Y.M.C.A.'s throughout the length and breadth of the land, and employ agents to buy up the artistic treasures of China for sepulture in their mansions. Chinese intellect, like that of America, will be, directly or indirectly, in the pay of the Trust magnates, and therefore no effective voice will be, raised in favour of radical reform. The inauguration of this system will be welcomed even by some Socialists in the West as a great victory for peace and freedom.

But it is impossible to make a silk purse out of a sow's ear, or peace and freedom out of capitalism. The fourfold agreement between England, France, America and Japan is, perhaps, a safeguard of peace, but in so far as it brings peace nearer it puts freedom further off. It is the peace obtained when competing firms join in a combine, which is by no means always advantageous to those who have profited by the previous competition. It is quite possible to dominate China without infringing the principle of the Open Door. This principle merely ensures that the domination everywhere shall be American, because America is the strongest Power financially and commercially. It is to America's interest to secure, in China, certain things consistent with Chinese interests, and certain others inconsistent with them. The Americans, for the sake of commerce and good investments, would wish to see a stable government in China, an increase in the purchasing power of the people, and an absence of territorial aggression by other Powers. But they will not wish to see the Chinese strong enough to own and work their own railways or mines, and they will resent all attempts at economic independence, particularly when (as is to be expected) they take the form of State Socialism, or what Lenin calls State Capitalism. They will keep a *dossier* of every student educated in colleges under American control, and will probably see to it that those who profess Socialist or Radical opinions shall get no posts. They will insist upon the standard of hypocrisy which led them to hound out Gorky when he visited the United States. They will destroy beauty and substitute tidiness. In short, they will insist upon China becoming as like as possible to "God's own country," except that it will not be allowed to keep the wealth generated by its industries. The Chinese have it in them to give to the world a new contribution to civilization as valuable as that which they gave in the past. This would be prevented by the domination of the Americans, because they believe their own civilization to be perfect.

The ideal of capitalism, if it could be achieved, would be to destroy competition among capitalists by means of Trusts, but to keep alive competition among workers. To some extent Trade Unionism has succeeded in diminishing competition among wage-earners within the advanced industrial countries; but it has only intensified the conflict between workers of different races, particularly between the white and yellow races.[7] Under the existing economic system, the competition of cheap Asiatic labour in America, Canada or Australia might well be harmful to white labour in those countries. But under Socialism an influx of industrious, skilled workers in sparsely populated countries would be an obvious gain to everybody. Under Socialism, the immigration of any person who produces more than he or she consumes will be a gain to every other individual in the community, since it increases the wealth per head. But under capitalism, owing to competition for jobs, a worker who either produces much or consumes little is the natural enemy of the others; thus the system makes for inefficient work, and creates an opposition between the general interest and the individual interest of the wage-earner. The case of yellow labour in America and the British Dominions is one of the most unfortunate instances of the artificial conflicts of interest produced by the capitalist system. This whole question of Asiatic immigration, which is liable to cause trouble for centuries to come, can only be radically solved by Socialism, since Socialism alone can bring the private interests of workers in this matter into harmony with the interests of their nation and of the world.

The concentration of the world's capital in a few nations, which, by means of it, are able to drain all other nations of their wealth, is obviously not a system by which permanent peace can be secured except through the complete subjection of the poorer nations. In the long run, China will see no reason to leave the profits of industry in the hands of foreigners. If, for the present, Russia is successfully starved into submission to foreign capital, Russia also will, when the time is ripe, attempt a new rebellion against the world-empire of finance. I cannot see, therefore, any establishment of a stable world-system as a result of the syndicate formed at Washington. On the contrary, we may expect that, when Asia has thoroughly assimilated our economic system, the Marxian class-war will break out in the form of a war between Asia and the West, with America as the protagonist of capitalism, and Russia as the champion of Asia and Socialism. In such a war, Asia would be fighting for freedom, but probably too late to preserve the distinctive civilizations which now make Asia valuable to the human family. Indeed, the war would probably be so devastating that no civilization of any sort would survive it.

To sum up: the real government of the world is in the hands of the big financiers, except on questions which rouse passionate public interest. No doubt the exclusion of Asiatics from America and the Dominions is due to popular pressure, and is against the interests of big finance. But not many questions rouse so much popular feeling, and among them only a few are sufficiently simple to be incapable of misrepresentation in the interests of the capitalists. Even in such a case as Asiatic immigration, it is the capitalist system which causes the anti-social interests of wage-earners and makes them illiberal. The existing system makes each man's individual interest opposed, in some vital point, to the interest of the whole. And what applies to individuals applies also to nations; under the existing economic system, a nation's interest is seldom the same as that of the world at large, and then only by accident. International peace might conceivably be secured under the present system, but only by a combination of the strong to exploit the weak. Such a combination is being attempted as the outcome of Washington; but it can only diminish, in the long run, the little freedom now enjoyed by the weaker nations.

The essential evil of the present system, as Socialists have pointed out over and over again, is production for profit instead of for use. A man or a company or a nation produces goods, not in order to consume them, but in order to sell them. Hence arise competition and exploitation and all the evils, both in internal labour problems and in international relations. The development of Chinese commerce by capitalistic methods means an increase, for the Chinese, in the prices of the things they export, which are also the things they chiefly consume, and the artificial stimulation of new needs for foreign goods, which places China at the mercy of those who supply these goods, destroys the existing contentment, and generates a feverish pursuit of purely material ends. In a socialistic world, production will be regulated by the same authority which represents the needs of the consumers, and the whole business of competitive buying and selling will cease. Until then, it is possible to have peace by submission to exploitation, or some degree of freedom by continual war, but it is not possible to have both peace and freedom. The success of the present American policy may, for a time, secure peace, but will certainly not secure freedom for the weaker nations, such as Chinese. Only international Socialism can secure both; and owing to the stimulation of revolt by capitalist oppression, even peace alone can never be secure until international Socialism is established throughout the world.

## NOTES

1 The interests of England, apart from the question of India, are roughly the same as those of America. Broadly speaking, British interests are allied with American finance, as against the pacifistic and agrarian tendencies of the Middle West.

2 It is interesting to observe that, since the Washington Conference, the American Administration has used the naval ratio there agreed upon to induce Congress to consent to a larger expenditure on the navy than would otherwise have been sanctioned. Expenditure on the navy is unpopular in America, but by its parade of pacifism the Government has been enabled to extract the necessary money out of the pockets of reluctant taxpayers. See *The Times'* New York Correspondent's telegram in *The Times* of April 10, 1922; also April 17 and 22.

3 See Chamberlain, *The Invention of a New Religion*, published by the Rationalist Press Association.

4 See Murdoch, *History of Japan*, I. pp. 500 ff.

5 An excellent account of these is given in *The Socialist and Labour Movement in Japan*, by an American Sociologist, published by the *Japan Chronicle*.

6 Author of a book called *If Japan and America Fight*.

7 The attitude of white labour to that of Asia is illustrated by the following telegram which appeared in *The Times* for April 5, 1922, from its Melbourne correspondent: "A deputation of shipwrights and allied trades complained to Mr. Hughes, the Prime Minister, that four Commonwealth ships had been repaired at Antwerp instead of in Australia, and that two had been repaired in India by black labour receiving eight annas (8d.) a day. When the deputation reached the black labour allegation Mr. Hughes jumped from his chair and turned on his interviewers with, ' Black labour be damned. Go to blithering blazes. Don't talk to me about black labour.' Hurrying from the room, he pushed his way through the deputation..." I do not generally agree with Mr. Hughes, but on this occasion, deeply as I deplore his language, I find myself in agreement with his sentiments, assuming that the phrase "black labour be damned" is meant to confer a blessing.

# 11

## CHINESE AND WESTERN CIVILIZATION CONTRASTED

There is at present in China, as we have seen in previous chapters, a close contact between our civilization and that which is native to the Celestial Empire. It is still a doubtful question whether this contact will breed a new civilization better than either of its parents, or whether it will merely destroy the native culture and replace it by that of America. Contacts between different civilizations have often in the past proved to be landmarks in human progress. Greece learnt from Egypt, Rome from Greece, the Arabs from the Roman Empire, mediaeval Europe from the Arabs, and Renaissance Europe from the Byzantines. In many of these cases, the pupils proved better than their masters. In the case of China, if we regard the Chinese as the pupils, this may be the case again. In fact, we have quite as much to learn from them as they from us, but there is far less chance of our learning it. If I treat the Chinese as our pupils, rather than vice versa, it is only because I fear we are unteachable.

I propose in this chapter to deal with the purely cultural aspects of the questions raised by the contact of China with the West. In the three following chapters, I shall deal with questions concerning the internal condition of China, returning finally, in a concluding chapter, to the hopes for the future which are permissible in the present difficult situation.

With the exception of Spain and America in the sixteenth century, I cannot think of any instance of two civilizations coming into contact after such a long period of separate development as has marked those of China and Europe. Considering this extraordinary separateness, it is surprising that mutual understanding between Europeans and Chinese is not more difficult. In order to make this point clear, it will be worth while to dwell for a moment on the historical origins of the two civilizations.

Western Europe and America have a practically homogeneous mental life, which I should trace to three sources: (1) Greek culture; (2) Jewish religion and ethics; (3) modern industrialism, which itself is an outcome of modern science. We may take Plato, the Old Testament, and Galileo as representing these three elements, which have remained singularly separable down to the present day. From the Greeks we derive literature and the arts, philosophy and pure mathematics; also the more urbane portions of our social outlook. From the Jews we derive fanatical belief, which its friends call "faith"; moral fervour, with the conception of sin; religious intolerance, and some part of our nationalism. From science, as applied in industrialism, we derive power and the sense of power, the belief that we are as gods, and may justly be the arbiters of life and death for unscientific races. We derive also the empirical method, by which almost all real knowledge has been acquired. These three elements, I think, account for most of our mentality.

No one of these three elements has had any appreciable part in the development of China, except that Greece indirectly influenced Chinese painting, sculpture, and music.[1] China belongs, in the dawn of its history, to the great river empires, of which Egypt and Babylonia contributed to our origins, by the influence which they had upon the Greeks and Jews. Just as these civilizations were rendered possible by the rich alluvial soil of the Nile, the Euphrates, and the Tigris, so the original civilization of China was rendered possible by the Yellow River. Even in the time of Confucius, the Chinese Empire did not stretch far either to south or north of the Yellow River. But in spite of this similarity in physical and economic circumstances, there was very little in common between the mental outlook of the Chinese and that of the Egyptians and Babylonians. Lao-Tze[2] and Confucius, who both belong to the sixth century B.C., have already the characteristics which we should regard as distinctive of the modern Chinese. People who attribute everything to economic causes would be hard put to it to account for the differences between the ancient Chinese and the ancient Egyptians and Babylonians. For my part, I have no alternative theory to offer. I do not think science can, at present, account wholly for national character. Climate and economic circumstances account for part, but not the whole. Probably a great deal depends upon the character of dominant individuals who happen to emerge at a formative period, such as Moses, Mahomet, and Confucius.

The oldest known Chinese sage is Lao-Tze, the founder of Taoism. "Lao-Tze" is not really a proper name, but means merely "the old philosopher." He was (according to tradition) an older contemporary of Confucius, and his philosophy is to my mind far more interesting. He held that every person, every animal, and every thing has a certain way or manner of behaving which is natural to him, or her, or it, and that we ought to conform to this way ourselves and encourage others to conform to it. "Tao" means "way," but used in a more or less mystical sense, as in the text: "I am the Way and the Truth and the Life." I think he fancied that death was due to departing from the "way," and that if we all lived strictly according to nature we should be immortal, like the heavenly bodies. In later times Taoism degenerated into mere magic, and was largely concerned with the search for the elixir of life. But I think the hope of escaping from death was an element in Taoist philosophy from the first.

Lao-Tze's book, or rather the book attributed to him, is very short, but his ideas were developed by his disciple Chuang-Tze, who is more interesting than his master. The philosophy which both advocated was one of freedom. They thought ill of government, and of all interferences with Nature. They complained of the hurry of modern life, which they contrasted with the calm existence of those whom they called "the pure men of old." There is a flavour of mysticism in the doctrine of the Tao, because in spite of the multiplicity of living things the Tao is in some sense one, so that if all live according to it there will be no strife in the world. But both sages have already the Chinese characteristics of humour, restraint, and under-statement. Their humour is illustrated by Chuang-Tze's account of Po-Lo who "understood the management of horses," and trained them till five out of every ten died.[3] Their restraint and under-statement are evident when they are compared with Western mystics. Both characteristics belong to all Chinese literature and art, and to the conversation of cultivated Chinese in the present day. All classes in China are fond of laughter, and never miss a chance of a joke. In the educated classes, the humour is sly and delicate, so that Europeans often fail to see it, which adds to the enjoyment of the Chinese. Their habit of under-statement is remarkable. I met one day in Peking a middle-aged man who told me he was academically interested in the theory of politics; being new to the country, I took his statement at its face value, but I afterwards discovered that he had been governor of a province, and had been for many years a very prominent politician. In Chinese poetry there is an apparent absence of passion which is due to the same practice of under-statement. They consider that a wise man should always remain calm, and though they have their passionate moments (being in fact a very excitable race), they do not wish to perpetuate them in art, because they think ill of them. Our romantic movement, which led people to like vehemence, has, so far as I know, no analogue in their literature. Their old music, some of which is very beautiful, makes so little noise that one can only just hear it. In art they aim at being exquisite, and in life at being reasonable. There is no admiration for the ruthless strong man, or for the unrestrained expression of passion. After the more blatant life of the West, one misses at first all the effects at which they are aiming; but gradually the beauty and dignity of their existence become visible, so that the foreigners who have lived longest in China are those who love the Chinese best.

The Taoists, though they survive as magicians, were entirely ousted from the favour of the educated classes by Confucianism. I must confess that I am unable to appreciate the merits of Confucius. His writings are largely occupied with trivial points of etiquette, and his main concern is to teach people how to behave correctly on various occasions. When one compares him, however, with the traditional religious teachers of some other ages and races, one must admit that he has great merits, even if they are mainly negative. His system, as developed by his followers, is one of pure ethics, without religious dogma; it has not given rise to a powerful priesthood, and it has not led to persecution. It certainly has succeeded in producing a whole nation possessed of exquisite manners and perfect courtesy. Nor is Chinese courtesy merely conventional; it is quite as reliable in situations for which no precedent has been provided. And it is not confined to one class; it exists even in the humblest coolie. It is humiliating to watch the brutal insolence of white men received by the Chinese with a quiet dignity which cannot demean itself to answer rudeness with rudeness. Europeans often regard this as weakness, but it is really strength, the strength by which the Chinese have hitherto conquered all their conquerors.

There is one, and only one, important foreign element in the traditional civilization of China, and that is Buddhism. Buddhism came to China from India in the early centuries of the Christian era, and acquired a definite place in the religion of the country. We, with the intolerant outlook which we have taken over from the Jews, imagine that if a man adopts one religion he cannot adopt another. The dogmas of Christianity and Mohammedanism, in their orthodox forms, are so framed that no man can accept both. But in China this incompatibility does not exist; a man may be both a Buddhist and a Confucian, because nothing in either is incompatible with the other. In Japan, similarly, most people are both Buddhists and Shintoists. Nevertheless there is a temperamental difference between Buddhism and Confucianism, which will cause any individual to lay stress on one or other even if he accepts both. Buddhism is a religion in the sense in which we understand the word. It has mystic doctrines and a way of salvation and a future life. It has a message to the world intended to cure the despair which it regards as natural to those who have no religious faith. It assumes an instinctive pessimism only to be cured by some gospel. Confucianism has nothing of all this. It assumes people [are] fundamentally at peace with the world, wanting only instruction as to how to live, not encouragement to live at all. And its ethical instruction is not based upon any metaphysical or religious dogma; it is purely mundane. The result of the co-existence of these two religions in China has been that the more religious and contemplative natures turned to Buddhism, while the active administrative type was content with Confucianism, which was always the official teaching, in which candidates for the civil service were examined. The result is that for many ages the Government of China has been in the hands of literary sceptics, whose administration has been lacking in those qualities of energy and destructiveness which Western nations demand of their rulers. In fact, they have conformed very closely to the maxims of Chuang-Tze. The result has been that the population has been happy except where civil war brought misery; that subject nations have been allowed autonomy; and that foreign nations have had no need to fear China, in spite of its immense population and resources.

Comparing the civilization of China with that of Europe, one finds in China most of what was to be found in Greece, but nothing of the other two elements of our civilization, namely Judaism and science. China is practically destitute of religion, not only in the upper classes, but throughout the population. There is a very definite ethical code, but it is not fierce or persecuting, and does not contain the notion "sin." Except quite recently, through European influence, there has been no science and no industrialism.

What will be the outcome of the contact of this ancient civilization with the West? I am not thinking of the political or economic outcome, but of the effect on the Chinese mental outlook. It is difficult to dissociate the two questions altogether, because of course the cultural contact with the West must be affected by the nature of the political and economic contact. Nevertheless, I wish to consider the cultural question as far as I can in isolation.

There is, in China, a great eagerness to acquire Western learning, not simply in order to acquire national strength and be able to resist Western aggression, but because a very large number of people consider learning a good thing in itself. It is traditional in China to place a high value on knowledge, but in old days the knowledge sought was only of the classical literature. Nowadays it is generally realized that Western knowledge is more useful. Many students go every year to universities in Europe, and still more to America, to learn science or economics or law or political theory. These men, when they return to China, mostly become teachers or civil servants or journalists or politicians. They are rapidly modernizing the Chinese outlook, especially in the educated classes.

The traditional civilization of China had become unprogressive, and had ceased to produce much of value in the way of art and literature. This was not due, I think, to any decadence in the race, but merely to lack of new material. The influx of Western knowledge provides just the stimulus that was needed. Chinese students are able and extraordinarily keen. Higher education suffers from lack of funds and absence of libraries, but does not suffer from any lack of the finest human material. Although Chinese civilization has hitherto been deficient in science, it never contained anything hostile to science, and therefore the spread of scientific knowledge encounters no such obstacles as the Church put in its way in Europe. I have no doubt that if the Chinese could get a stable government and sufficient funds, they would, within the next thirty years, begin to produce remarkable work in science. It is quite likely that they might outstrip us, because they come with fresh zest and with all the ardour of a renaissance. In fact, the enthusiasm for learning in Young China reminds one constantly of the renaissance spirit in fifteenth-century Italy.

It is very remarkable, as distinguishing the Chinese from the Japanese, that the things they wish to learn from us are not those that bring wealth or military strength, but rather those that have either an ethical and social value, or a purely intellectual interest. They are not by any means uncritical of our civilization. Some of them told me that they were less critical before 1914, but that the war made them think there must be imperfections in the Western manner of life. The habit of looking to the West for wisdom was, however, very strong, and some of the younger ones thought that Bolshevism could give what they were looking for. That hope also must be suffering disappointment, and before long they will realize that they must work out their own salvation by means of a new synthesis. The Japanese adopted our faults and kept their own, but it is possible to hope that the Chinese will make the opposite selection, keeping their own merits and adopting ours.

The distinctive merit of our civilization, I should say, is the scientific method; the distinctive merit of the Chinese is a just conception of the ends of life. It is these two that one must hope to see gradually uniting.

Lao-Tze describes the operation of Tao as "production without possession, action without self-assertion, development without domination." I think one could derive from these words a conception of the ends of life as reflective Chinese see them, and it must be admitted that they are very different from the ends which most white men set before themselves. Possession, self-assertion, domination, are eagerly sought, both nationally and individually. They have been erected into a philosophy by Nietzsche, and Nietzsche's disciples are not confined to Germany.

But, it will be said, you have been comparing Western practice with Chinese theory; if you had compared Western theory with Chinese practice, the balance would have come out quite differently. There is, of course, a great deal of truth in this. Possession, which is one of the three things that Lao-Tze wishes us to forego, is certainly dear to the heart of the average Chinaman. As a race, they are tenacious of money—not perhaps more so than the French, but certainly more than the English or the Americans. Their politics are corrupt, and their powerful men make money in disgraceful ways. All this it is impossible to deny.

Nevertheless, as regards the other two evils, self-assertion and domination, I notice a definite superiority to ourselves in Chinese practice. There is much less desire than among the white races to tyrannize over other people. The weakness of China internationally is quite as much due to this virtue as to the vices of corruption and so on which are usually assigned as the sole reason. If any nation in the world could ever be "too proud to fight," that nation would be China. The natural Chinese attitude is one of tolerance and friendliness, showing courtesy and expecting it in return. If the Chinese chose, they could be the most powerful nation in the world. But they only desire freedom, not domination. It is not improbable that other nations may compel them to fight for their freedom, and if so, they may lose their virtues and acquire a taste for empire. But at present, though they have been an imperial race for 2,000 years, their love of empire is extraordinarily slight.

Although there have been many wars in China, the natural outlook of the Chinese is very pacifistic. I do not know of any other country where a poet would have chosen, as Po-Chui did in one of the poems translated by Mr. Waley, called by him *The Old Man with the Broken Arm*, to make a hero of a recruit who maimed himself to escape military service. Their pacifism is rooted in their contemplative outlook, and in the fact that they do not desire to change whatever they see. They take a pleasure—as their pictures show—in observing characteristic manifestations of different kinds of life, and they have no wish to reduce everything to a preconceived pattern. They have not the ideal of progress which dominates the Western nations, and affords a rationalization of our active impulses. Progress is, of course, a very modern ideal even with us; it is part of what we owe to science and industrialism. The cultivated conservative Chinese of the present day talk exactly as their earliest sages write. If one points out to them that this shows how little progress there has been, they will say: "Why seek progress when you already enjoy what is excellent?" At first, this point of view seems to a European unduly indolent; but gradually doubts as to one's own wisdom grow up, and one begins to think that much of what we call progress is only restless change, bringing us no nearer to any desirable goal.

It is interesting to contrast what the Chinese have sought in the West with what the West has sought in China. The Chinese in the West seek knowledge, in the hope—which I fear is usually [in] vain—that knowledge may prove a gateway to wisdom. White men have gone to China with three motives: to fight, to make money, and to convert the Chinese to our religion. The last of these motives has the merit of being idealistic, and has inspired many heroic lives. But the soldier, the merchant, and the missionary are alike concerned to stamp our civilization upon the world; they are all three, in a certain sense, pugnacious. The Chinese have no wish to convert us to Confucianism; they say "religions are many, but reason is one," and with that they are content to let us go our way. They are good merchants, but their methods are quite different from those of European merchants in China, who are perpetually seeking concessions, monopolies, railways, and mines, and endeavouring to get their claims supported by gunboats. The Chinese are not, as a rule, good soldiers, because the causes for which they are asked to fight are not worth fighting for, and they know it. But that is only a proof of their reasonableness.

I think the tolerance of the Chinese is in excess of anything that Europeans can imagine from their experience at home. We imagine ourselves tolerant, because we are more so than our ancestors. But we still practise political and social persecution, and what is more, we are firmly persuaded that our civilization and our way of life are immeasurably better than any other, so that when we come across a nation like the Chinese, we are convinced that the kindest thing we can do to them is to make them like ourselves. I believe this to be a profound mistake. It seemed to me that the average Chinaman, even if he is miserably poor, is happier than the average Englishman, and is happier because the nation is built upon a more humane and civilized outlook than our own. Restlessness and pugnacity not only cause obvious evils, but fill our lives with discontent, incapacitate us for the enjoyment of beauty, and make us almost incapable of the contemplative virtues. In this respect we have grown rapidly worse during the last hundred years. I do not deny that the Chinese go too far in the other direction; but for that very reason I think contact between East and West is likely to be fruitful to both parties. They may learn from us the indispensable minimum of practical efficiency, and we may learn from them something of that contemplative wisdom which has enabled them to persist while all the other nations of antiquity have perished.

When I went to China, I went to teach; but every day that I stayed I thought less of what I had to teach them and more of what I had to learn from them. Among Europeans who had lived a long time in China, I found this attitude not uncommon; but among those whose stay is short, or who go only to make money, it is sadly rare. It is rare because the Chinese do not excel in the things we really value— military prowess and industrial enterprise. But those who value wisdom or beauty, or even the simple enjoyment of life, will find more of these things in China than in the distracted and turbulent West, and will be happy to live where such things are valued. I wish I could hope that China, in return for our scientific knowledge, may give us something of her large tolerance and contemplative peace of mind.

## NOTES

1   See Cordier, op. cit. i. p. 368, and Giles, op. cit. p. 187.
2   With regard to Lao-Tze, the book which bears his name is of doubtful authenticity, and was probably compiled two or three centuries after his death. Cf. Giles, op. cit., Lecture V.
3   Quoted in Chap. IV, pp. 82–3.

# 12

## THE CHINESE CHARACTER

There is a theory among Occidentals that the Chinaman is inscrutable, full of secret thoughts, and impossible for us to understand. It may be that a greater experience of China would have brought me to share this opinion; but I could see nothing to support it during the time when I was working in that country. I talked to the Chinese as I should have talked to English people, and they answered me much as English people would have answered a Chinese whom they considered educated and not wholly unintelligent. I do not believe in the myth of the "Subtle Oriental": I am convinced that in a game of mutual deception an Englishman or American can beat a Chinese nine times out of ten. But as many comparatively poor Chinese have dealings with rich white men, the game is often played only on one side. Then, no doubt, the white man is deceived and swindled; but not more than a Chinese mandarin would be in London.

One of the most remarkable things about the Chinese is their power of securing the affection of foreigners. Almost all Europeans like China, both those who come only as tourists and those who live there for many years. In spite of the Anglo-Japanese Alliance, I can re-call hardly a single Englishman in the Far East who liked the Japanese as well as the Chinese. Those who have lived long among them tend to acquire their outlook and their standards. New arrivals are struck by obvious evils: the beggars, the terrible poverty, the prevalence of disease, the anarchy and corruption in politics. Every energetic West-erner feels at first a strong desire to reform these evils, and of course they ought to be reformed.

But the Chinese, even those who are the victims of preventable mis-fortunes, show a vast passive indifference to the excitement of the for-eigners; they wait for it to go off, like the effervescence of soda-water. And gradually strange hesitations creep into the mind of the bewil-dered traveller; after a period of indignation, he begins to doubt all the maxims he has hitherto accepted without question. Is it really wise to be always guarding against future misfortune? Is it prudent to lose all enjoyment of the present through thinking of the disasters that may come at some future date? Should our lives be passed in building a mansion that we shall never have leisure to inhabit?

The Chinese answer these questions in the negative, and therefore have to put up with poverty, disease, and anarchy. But, to compensate for these evils, they have retained, as industrial nations have not, the capacity for civilized enjoyment, for leisure and laughter, for pleasure in sunshine and philosophical discourse. The Chinese, of all classes, are more laughter-loving than any other race with which I am acquainted; they find amusement in everything, and a dispute can always be sof-tened by a joke.

I remember one hot day when a party of us were crossing the hills in chairs—the way was rough and very steep, the work for the coolies very severe. At the highest point of our journey, we stopped for ten minutes to let the men rest. Instantly they all sat in a row, brought out their pipes, and began to laugh among themselves as if they had not a care in the world. In any country that had learned the virtue of forethought, they would have devoted the moments to complaining of the heat, in order to increase their tip. We, being Europeans, spent the time worrying whether the automobile would be waiting for us at the right place. Well-to-do Chinese would have started a discussion as to whether the universe moves in cycles or progresses by a rectilinear motion; or they might have set to work to consider whether the truly virtuous man shows *complete* self-abnegation, or may, on occasion, consider his own interest.

One comes across white men occasionally who suffer under the delusion that China is not a civilized country. Such men have quite forgotten what constitutes civilization. It is true that there are no trams in Peking, and that the electric light is poor. It is true that there are places full of beauty, which Europeans itch to make hideous by digging up coal. It is true that the educated Chinaman is better at writing poetry than at remembering the sort of facts which can be looked up in *Whitaker's Almanac*. A European, in recommending a place of residence, will tell you that it has a good train service; the best quality he can conceive in any place is that it should be easy to get away from. But a Chinaman will tell you nothing about the trains; if you ask, he will tell you wrong. What he tells you is that there is a palace built by an ancient emperor, and a retreat in a lake for scholars weary of the world, founded by a famous poet of the Tang dynasty. It is this outlook that strikes the Westerner as barbaric.

The Chinese, from the highest to the lowest, have an imperturbable quiet dignity, which is usually not destroyed even by a European education. They are not self-assertive, either individually or nationally; their pride is too profound for self-assertion. They admit China's military weakness in comparison with foreign Powers, but they do not consider efficiency in homicide the most important quality in a man or a nation. I think that, at bottom, they almost all believe that China is the greatest nation in the world, and has the finest civilization. A Westerner cannot be expected to accept this view, because it is based on traditions utterly different from his own. But gradually one comes to feel that it is, at any rate, not an absurd view; that it is, in fact, the logical outcome of a self-consistent standard of values. The typical Westerner wishes to be the cause of as many changes as possible in his environment; the typical Chinaman wishes to enjoy as much and as delicately as possible. This difference is at the bottom of most of the contrast between China and the English-speaking world.

We in the West make a fetish of "progress," which is the ethical camouflage of the desire to be the cause of changes. If we are asked, for instance, whether machinery has really improved the world, the question strikes us as foolish: it has brought great changes and therefore great "progress." What we believe to be a love of progress is really, in nine cases out of ten, a love of power, an enjoyment of the feeling that by our fiat we can make things different. For the sake of this pleasure, a young American will work so hard that, by the time he has acquired his millions, he has become a victim of dyspepsia, compelled to live on toast and water, and to be a mere spectator of the feasts that he offers to his guests. But he consoles himself with the thought that he can control politics, and provoke or prevent wars as may suit his investments. It is this temperament that makes Western nations "progressive."

There are, of course, ambitious men in China, but they are less common than among ourselves. And their ambition takes a different form—not a better form, but one produced by the preference of enjoyment to power. It is a natural result of this preference that avarice is a widespread failing of the Chinese. Money brings the means of enjoyment, therefore money is passionately desired. With us, money is desired chiefly as a means to power; politicians, who can acquire power without much money, are often content to remain poor. In China, the tuchuns (military governors), who have the real power, almost always use it for the sole purpose of amassing a fortune. Their object is to escape to Japan at a suitable moment, with sufficient plunder to enable them to enjoy life quietly for the rest of their days. The fact that in escaping they lose power does not trouble them in the least. It is, of course, obvious that such politicians, who spread devastation only in the provinces committed to their care, are far less harmful to the world than our own, who ruin whole continents in order to win an election campaign.

The corruption and anarchy in Chinese politics do much less harm than one would be inclined to expect. But for the predatory desires of the Great Powers—especially Japan—the harm would be much less than is done by our own "efficient" Governments. Nine-tenths of the activities of a modern Government are harmful; therefore the worse they are performed, the better. In China, where the Government is lazy, corrupt, and stupid, there is a degree of individual liberty which has been wholly lost in the rest of the world.

The laws are just as bad as elsewhere; occasionally, under foreign pressure, a man is imprisoned for Bolshevist propaganda, just as he might be in England or America. But this is quite exceptional; as a rule, in practice, there is very little interference with free speech and a free Press.[1] The individual does not feel obliged to follow the herd, as he has in Europe since 1914, and in America since 1917. Men still think for themselves, and are not afraid to announce the conclusions at which they arrive. Individualism has perished in the West, but in China it survives, for good as well as for evil. Self-respect and personal dignity are possible for every coolie in China, to a degree which is, among ourselves, possible only for a few leading financiers.

The business of "saving face," which often strikes foreigners in China as ludicrous, is only the carrying-out of respect for personal dignity in the sphere of social manners. Everybody has "face," even the humblest beggar; there are humiliations that you must not inflict upon him, if you are not to outrage the Chinese ethical code. If you speak to a Chinaman in a way that transgresses the code, he will laugh, because your words must be taken as spoken in jest if they are not to constitute an offence.

Once I thought that the students to whom I was lecturing were not as industrious as they might be, and I told them so in just the same words that I should have used to English students in the same circumstances. But I soon found I was making a mistake. They all laughed uneasily, which surprised me until I saw the reason. Chinese life, even among the most modernized, is far more polite than anything to which we are accustomed. This, of course, interferes with efficiency, and also (what is more serious) with sincerity and truth in personal relations. If I were Chinese, I should wish to see it mitigated. But to those who suffer from the brutalities of the West, Chinese urbanity is very restful. Whether on the balance it is better or worse than our frankness, I shall not venture to decide.

The Chinese remind one of the English in their love of compromise and in their habit of bowing to public opinion. Seldom is a conflict pushed to its ultimate brutal issue. The treatment of the Manchu Emperor may be taken as a case in point. When a Western country becomes a Republic, it is customary to cut off the head of the deposed monarch, or at least to cause him to fly the country. But the Chinese have left the Emperor his title, his beautiful palace, his troops of eunuchs, and an income of several million dollars a year. He is a boy of sixteen, living peaceably in the Forbidden City. Once, in the course of a civil war, he was nominally restored to power for a few days; but he was deposed again, without being in any way punished for the use to which he had been put.

Public opinion is a very real force in China, when it can be roused. It was, by all accounts, mainly responsible for the downfall of the An Fu party in the summer of 1920. This party was pro-Japanese and was accepting loans from Japan. Hatred of Japan is the strongest and most widespread of political passions in China, and it was stirred up by the students in fiery orations. The An Fu party had, at first, a great preponderance of military strength; but their soldiers melted away when they came to understand the cause for which they were expected to fight. In the end, the opponents of the An Fu party were able to enter Peking and change the Government almost without firing a shot.

The same influence of public opinion was decisive in the teachers' strike, which was on the point of being settled when I left Peking. The Government, which is always impecunious, owing to corruption, had left its teachers unpaid for many months. At last they struck to enforce payment, and went on a peaceful deputation to the Government, accompanied by many students. There was a clash with the soldiers and police, and many teachers and students were more or less severely wounded. This led to a terrific outcry, because the love of education in China is profound and widespread. The newspapers clamoured for revolution. The Government had just spent nine million dollars in corrupt payments to three Tuchuns who had descended upon the capital to extort blackmail. It could not find any colourable pretext for refusing the few hundred thousands required by the teachers, and it capitulated in panic. I do not think there is any Anglo-Saxon country where the interests of teachers would have roused the same degree of public feeling.

Nothing astonishes a European more in the Chinese than their patience. The educated Chinese are well aware of the foreign menace. They realize acutely what the Japanese have done in Manchuria and Shantung. They are aware that the English in Hong-Kong are doing their utmost to bring to naught the Canton attempt to introduce good government in the South. They know that all the Great Powers, without exception, look with greedy eyes upon the undeveloped resources of their country, especially its coal and iron. They have before them the example of Japan, which, by developing a brutal militarism, a cast-iron discipline, and a new reactionary religion, has succeeded in holding at bay the fierce lusts of "civilized" industrialists. Yet they neither copy Japan nor submit tamely to foreign domination. They think not in decades, but in centuries. They have been conquered before, first by the Tartars and then by the Manchus; but in both cases they absorbed their conquerors. Chinese civilization persisted, unchanged; and after a few generations the invaders became more Chinese than their subjects.

Manchuria is a rather empty country, with abundant room for colonization. The Japanese assert that they need colonies for their surplus population, yet the Chinese immigrants into Manchuria exceed the Japanese a hundredfold. Whatever may be the temporary political status of Manchuria, it will remain a part of Chinese civilization, and can be recovered whenever Japan happens to be in difficulties. The Chinese derive such strength from their four hundred millions, the toughness of their national customs, their power of passive resistance, and their unrivalled national cohesiveness—in spite of the civil wars, which merely ruffle the surface—that they can afford to despise military methods, and to wait till the feverish energy of their oppressors shall have exhausted itself in internecine combats.

China is much less a political entity than a civilization—the only one that has survived from ancient times. Since the days of Confucius, the Egyptian, Babylonian, Persian, Macedonian, and Roman Empires have perished; but China has persisted through a continuous evolution. There have been foreign influences—first Buddhism, and now Western science. But Buddhism did not turn the Chinese into Indians, and Western science will not turn them into Europeans. I have met men in China who knew as much of Western learning as any professor among ourselves; yet they had not been thrown off their balance, or lost touch with their own people. What is bad in the West—its brutality, its restlessness, its readiness to oppress the weak, its preoccupation with purely material aims—they see to be bad, and do not wish to adopt. What is good, especially its science, they do wish to adopt.

The old indigenous culture of China has become rather dead; its art and literature are not what they were, and Confucius does not satisfy the spiritual needs of a modern man, even if he is Chinese. The Chinese who have had a European or American education realize that a new element is needed to vitalize native traditions, and they look to our civilization to supply it. But they do not wish to construct a civilization just like ours; and it is precisely in this that the best hope lies. If they are not goaded into militarism, they may produce a genuinely new civilization, better than any that we in the West have been able to create.

So far, I have spoken chiefly of the good sides of the Chinese character; but of course China, like every other nation, has its bad sides also. It is disagreeable to me to speak of these, as I experienced so much courtesy and real kindness from the Chinese, that I should prefer to say only nice things about them. But for the sake of China, as well as for the sake of truth, it would be a mistake to conceal what is less admirable. I will only ask the reader to remember that, on the balance, I think the Chinese one of the best nations I have come across, and am prepared to draw up a graver indictment against every one of the Great Powers. Shortly before I left China, an eminent Chinese writer pressed me to say what I considered the chief defects of the Chinese. With some reluctance, I mentioned three: avarice, cowardice, and callousness. Strange to say, my interlocutor, instead of getting angry, admitted the justice of my criticism, and proceeded to discuss possible remedies. This is a sample of the intellectual integrity which is one of China's greatest virtues.

The callousness of the Chinese is bound to strike every Anglo-Saxon. They have none of that humanitarian impulse which leads us to devote one per cent of our energy to mitigating the evils wrought by the other ninety-nine per cent. For instance, we have been forbidding the Austrians to join with Germany, to emigrate, or to obtain the raw materials of industry. Therefore the Viennese have starved, except those whom it has pleased us to keep alive from philanthropy. The Chinese would not have had the energy to starve the Viennese, or the philanthropy to keep some of them alive. While I was in China, millions were dying of famine; men sold their children into slavery for a few dollars, and killed them if this sum was unobtainable. Much was done by white men to relieve the famine, but very little by the Chinese, and that little vitiated by corruption. It must be said, however, that the efforts of the white men were more effective in soothing their own consciences than in helping the Chinese. So long as the present birth-rate and the present methods of agriculture persist, famines are bound to occur periodically; and those whom philanthropy keeps alive through one famine are only too likely to perish in the next.

Famines in China can be permanently cured only by better methods of agriculture combined with emigration or birth-control on a large scale. Educated Chinese realize this, and it makes them indifferent to efforts to keep the present victims alive. A great deal of Chinese callousness has a similar explanation, and is due to perception of the vastness of the problems involved. But there remains a residue which cannot be so explained. If a dog is run over by an automobile and seriously hurt, nine out of ten passers-by will stop to laugh at the poor brute's howls. The spectacle of suffering does not of itself rouse any sympathetic pain in the average Chinaman; in fact, he seems to find it mildly agreeable. Their history, and their penal code before the revolution of 1911, show that they are by no means destitute of the impulse of active cruelty; but of this I did not myself come across any instances. And it must be said that active cruelty is practised by all the great nations, to an extent concealed from us only by our hypocrisy.

Cowardice is prima facie a fault of the Chinese; but I am not sure that they are really lacking in courage. It is true that, in battles between rival tuchuns, both sides run away, and victory rests with the side that first discovers the flight of the other. But this proves only that the Chinese soldier is a rational man. No cause of any importance is involved, and the armies consist of mere mercenaries. When there is a serious issue, as, for instance, in the Tai-Ping rebellion, the Chinese are said to fight well, particularly if they have good officers. Nevertheless, I do not think that, in comparison with the Anglo-Saxons, the French, or the Germans, the Chinese can be considered a courageous people, except in the matter of passive endurance. They will endure torture, and even death, for motives which men of more pugnacious races would find insufficient—for example, to conceal the hiding-place of stolen plunder. In spite of their comparative lack of *active* courage, they have less fear of death than we have, as is shown by their readiness to commit suicide.

Avarice is, I should say, the gravest defect of the Chinese. Life is hard, and money is not easily obtained. For the sake of money, all except a very few foreign-educated Chinese will be guilty of corruption. For the sake of a few pence, almost any coolie will run an imminent risk of death. The difficulty of combating Japan has arisen mainly from the fact that hardly any Chinese politician can resist Japanese bribes. I think this defect is probably due to the fact that, for many ages, an honest living has been hard to get; in which case it will be lessened as economic conditions improve. I doubt if it is any worse now in China than it was in Europe in the eighteenth century. I have not heard of any Chinese general more corrupt than Marlborough, or of any politician more corrupt than Cardinal Dubois. It is, therefore, quite likely that changed industrial conditions will make the Chinese as honest as we are—which is not saying much.

I have been speaking of the Chinese as they are in ordinary life, when they appear as men of active and sceptical intelligence, but of somewhat sluggish passions. There is, however, another side to them: they are capable of wild excitement, often of a collective kind. I saw little of this myself, but there can be no doubt of the fact. The Boxer rising was a case in point, and one which particularly affected Europeans. But their history is full of more or less analogous disturbances. It is this element in their character that makes them incalculable, and makes it impossible even to guess at their future. One can imagine a section of them becoming fanatically Bolshevist, or anti-Japanese, or Christian, or devoted to some leader who would ultimately declare himself Emperor. I suppose it is this element in their character that makes them, in spite of their habitual caution, the most reckless gamblers in the world. And many emperors have lost their thrones through the force of romantic love, although romantic love is far more despised than it is in the West.

To sum up the Chinese character is not easy. Much of what strikes the foreigner is due merely to the fact that they have preserved an ancient civilization which is not industrial. All this is likely to pass away, under the pressure of the Japanese, and of European and American financiers. Their art is already perishing, and being replaced by crude imitations of second-rate European pictures. Most of the Chinese who have had a European education are quite incapable of seeing any beauty in native painting, and merely observe contemptuously that it does not obey the laws of perspective.

The obvious charm which the tourist finds in China cannot be preserved; it must perish at the touch of industrialism. But perhaps something may be preserved, something of the ethical qualities in which China is supreme, and which the modern world most desperately needs. Among these qualities I place first the pacific temper, which seeks to settle disputes on grounds of justice rather than by force. It remains to be seen whether the West will allow this temper to persist, or will force it to give place, in self-defence, to a frantic militarism like that to which Japan has been driven.

## NOTE

1    This vexes the foreigners, who are attempting to establish a very severe Press censorship in Shanghai. See "The Shanghai Printed Matter Bye-Law." Hollington K. Tong, *Review of the Far East*, April 15, 1922.

# 13

# HIGHER EDUCATION IN CHINA

China, like Italy and Greece, is frequently misjudged by persons of culture because they regard it as a museum. The preservation of ancient beauty is very important, but no vigorous forward-looking man is content to be a mere curator. The result is that the best people in China tend to be Philistines as regards all that is pleasing to the European tourist. The European in China, quite apart from interested motives, is apt to be ultra-conservative, because he likes everything distinctive and non-European. But this is the attitude of an outsider, of one who regards China as a country to be looked at rather than lived in, as a country with a past rather than a future. Patriotic Chinese naturally do not view their country in this way; they wish their country to acquire what is best in the modern world, not merely to remain an interesting survival of a by-gone age, like Oxford or the Yellowstone Park. As the first step to this end, they do all they can to promote higher education, and to increase the number of Chinese who can use and appreciate Western knowledge without being the slaves of Western follies.

What is being done in this direction is very interesting, and one of the most hopeful things happening in our not very cheerful epoch.

There is first the old traditional curriculum, the learning by rote of the classics without explanation in early youth, followed by a more intelligent study in later years. This is exactly like the traditional study of the classics in this country, as it existed, for example, in the eighteenth century. Men over thirty, even if, in the end, they have secured a thoroughly modern education, have almost all begun by learning reading and writing in old-fashioned schools. Such schools still form the majority, and give most of the elementary education that is given. Every child has to learn by heart every day some portion of the classical text, and repeat it out loud in class. As they all repeat at the same time, the din is deafening. (In Peking I lived next to one of these schools, so I can speak from experience.) The number of people who are taught to read by these methods is considerable; in the large towns one finds that even coolies can read as often as not. But writing (which is very difficult in Chinese) is a much rarer accomplishment. Probably those who can both read and write form about five per cent of the population.

The establishment of normal schools for the training of teachers on modern lines, which grew out of the edict of 1905 abolishing the old examination system and proclaiming the need of educational reform, has done much, and will do much more, to transform and extend elementary education. The following statistics showing the increase in the number of schools, teachers, and students in China are taken from Mr. Tyau's *China Awakened*, p. 4:—

|  | 1910 | 1914 | 1917 | 1919 |
|---|---|---|---|---|
| Number of Schools | 42,444 | 59,796 | 128,048 | 134,000 |
| Number of Teachers | 185,566 | 200,000 | 326,417 | 326,000 |
| Number of Students | 1,625,534 | 3,849,554 | 4,269,197 | 4,500,000 |

Considering that the years concerned are years of revolution and civil war, it must be admitted that the progress shown by these figures is very remarkable.

There are schemes for universal elementary education, but so far, owing to the disturbed condition of the country and the lack of funds, it has been impossible to carry them out except in a few places on a small scale. They would, however, be soon carried out if there were a stable government.

The traditional classical education was, of course, not intended to be only elementary. The amount of Chinese literature is enormous, and the older texts are extremely difficult to understand. There is scope, within the tradition, for all the industry and erudition of the finest renaissance scholars. Learning of this sort has been respected in China for many ages. One meets old scholars of this type, to whose opinions, even in politics, it is customary to defer, although they have the innocence and unworldliness of the old-fashioned don. They remind one almost of the men whom Lamb describes in his essay on Oxford in the Vacation—learned, lovable, and sincere, but utterly lost in the modern world, basing their opinions of Socialism, for example, on what some eleventh-century philosopher said about it. The arguments for and against the type of higher education that they represent are exactly the same as those for and against a classical education in Europe, and one is driven to the same conclusion in both cases: that the existence of specialists having this type of knowledge is highly desirable, but that the ordinary curriculum for the average educated person should take more account of modern needs, and give more instruction in science, modern languages, and contemporary international relations. This is the view, so far as I could discover, of all reforming educationists in China.

The second kind of higher education in China is that initiated by the missionaries, and now almost entirely in the hands of the Americans. As everyone knows, America's position in Chinese education was acquired through the Boxer indemnity. Most of the Powers, at that time, if their own account is to be believed, demanded a sum representing only actual loss and damage, but the Americans, according to their critics, demanded (and obtained) a vastly larger sum, of which they generously devoted the surplus to educating Chinese students, both in China and at American universities. This course of action has abundantly justified itself, both politically and commercially; a larger and larger number of posts in China go to men who have come under American influence, and who have come to believe that America is the one true friend of China among the Great Powers.

One may take as typical of American work three institutions of which I saw a certain amount: Tsing-Hua College (about ten miles from Peking), the Peking Union Medical College (connected with the Rockefeller Hospital), and the so-called Peking University.

Tsing-Hua College, delightfully situated at the foot of the Western hills, with a number of fine solid buildings, [1] in a good American style, owes its existence entirely to the Boxer indemnity money.

It has an atmosphere exactly like that of a small American university, and a (Chinese) President who is an almost perfect reproduction of the American College President. The teachers are partly American, partly Chinese educated in America, and there tends to be more and more of the latter. As one enters the gates, one becomes aware of the presence of every virtue usually absent in China: cleanliness, punctuality, exactitude, efficiency. I had not much opportunity to judge of the teaching, but whatever I saw made me think that the institution was thorough and good. One great merit, which belongs to American institutions generally, is that the students are made to learn English. Chinese differs so profoundly from European languages that even with the most skilful translations a student who knows only Chinese cannot understand European ideas; therefore the learning of some European language is essential, and English is far the most familiar and useful throughout the Far East.

The students at Tsing-Hua College learn mathematics and science and philosophy, and broadly speaking, the more elementary parts of what is commonly taught in universities. Many of the best of them go afterwards to America, where they take a Doctor's degree. On returning to China they become teachers or civil servants. Undoubtedly they contribute greatly to the improvement of their country in efficiency and honesty and technical intelligence.

The Rockefeller Hospital is a large, conspicuous building, representing an interesting attempt to combine something of Chinese beauty with European utilitarian requirements. The green roofs are quite Chinese, but the walls and windows are European. The attempt is praiseworthy, though perhaps not wholly successful. The hospital has all the most modern scientific apparatus, but, with the monopolistic tendency of the Standard Oil Company, it refuses to let its apparatus be of use to anyone not connected with the hospital. The Peking Union Medical College teaches many things besides medicine—English literature, for example—and apparently teaches them well. They are necessary in order to produce Chinese physicians and surgeons who will reach the European level, because a good knowledge of some European language is necessary for medicine as for other kinds of European learning. And a sound knowledge of scientific medicine is, of course, of immense importance to China, where there is no sort of sanitation and epidemics are frequent.

The so-called Peking University is an example of what the Chinese have to suffer on account of extra-territoriality. The Chinese Government (so at least I was told) had already established a university in Peking, fully equipped and staffed, and known as the Peking University. But the Methodist missionaries decided to give the name "Peking University" to their schools, so the already existing university had to alter its name to "Government University." The case is exactly as if a collection of old-fashioned Chinamen had established themselves in London to teach the doctrine of Confucius, and had been able to force London University to abandon its name to them. However, I do not wish to raise the question of extra-territoriality, the more so as I do not think it can be abandoned for some years to come, in spite of the abuses to which it sometimes gives rise.

Returned students (i.e. students who have been at foreign universities) form a definite set in China.[2] There is in Peking a "Returned Students' Club," a charming place. It is customary among Europeans to speak ill of returned students, but for no good reason. There are occasionally disagreements between different sections; in particular, those who have been only to Japan are not regarded quite as equals by those who have been to Europe or America. My impression was that America puts a more definite stamp upon a student than any other country; certainly those returning from England are less Anglicized than those returning from the United States are Americanized. To the Chinaman who wishes to be modern and up-to-date, skyscrapers and hustle seem romantic, because they are so unlike his home. The old traditions which conservative Europeans value are such a mushroom growth compared to those of China (where authentic descendants of Confucius abound) that it is useless to attempt that way of impressing the Chinese. One is reminded of the conversation in *Eothen* between the English country gentleman and the Pasha, in which the Pasha praises England to the refrain: "Buzz, buzz, all by steam; whir, whir, all on wheels," while the Englishman keeps saying: "Tell the Pasha that the British yeoman is still, thank God, the British yeoman."

Although the educational work of the Americans in China is on the whole admirable, nothing directed by foreigners can adequately satisfy the needs of the country. The Chinese have a civilization and a national temperament in many ways superior to those of white men. A few Europeans ultimately discover this, but Americans never do. They remain always missionaries—not of Christianity, though they often think that is what they are preaching, but of Americanism. What is Americanism? "Clean living, clean thinking, and pep," I think an American would reply. This means, in practice, the substitution of ti-diness for art, cleanliness for beauty, moralizing for philosophy, pros-titutes for concubines (as being easier to conceal), and a general air of being fearfully busy for the leisurely calm of the traditional Chinese. Voltaire—that hardened old cynic—laid it down that the true ends of life are "*aimer et penser.*" Both are common in China, but neither is compatible with "pep." The American influence, therefore, inevitably tends to eliminate both. If it prevailed it would, no doubt, by means of hygiene, save the lives of many Chinamen, but would at the same time make them not worth saving. It cannot therefore be regarded as wholly and altogether satisfactory.

The best Chinese educationists are aware of this, and have estab-lished schools and universities which are modern but under Chinese direction. In these, a certain proportion of the teachers are European or American, but the spirit of the teaching is not that of the Y.M.C.A.

One can never rid oneself of the feeling that the education controlled by white men is not disinterested; it seems always designed, unconsciously in the main, to produce convenient tools for the capitalist penetration of China by the merchants and manufacturers of the nation concerned. Modern Chinese schools and universities are singularly different: they are not hotbeds of rabid nationalism as they would be in any other country, but institutions where the student is taught to think freely, and his thoughts are judged by their intelligence, not by their utility to exploiters. The outcome, among the best young men, is a really beautiful intellectual disinterestedness. The discussions which I used to have in my seminar (consisting of students belonging to the Peking Government University) could not have been surpassed anywhere for keenness, candour, and fearlessness. I had the same impression of the Science Society of Nanking, and of all similar bodies wherever I came across them. There is, among the young, a passionate desire to acquire Western knowledge, together with a vivid realization of Western vices. They wish to be scientific but not mechanical, industrial but not capitalistic. To a man they are Socialists, as are most of the best among their Chinese teachers. They respect the knowledge of Europeans, but quietly put aside their arrogance. For the present, the purely Chinese modern educational institutions, such as the Peking Government University, leave much to be desired from the point of view of instruction; there are no adequate libraries, the teaching of English is not sufficiently thorough, and there is not enough mental discipline. But these are the faults of youth, and are unimportant compared with the profoundly humanistic attitude to life which is formed in the students. Most of the faults may be traced to the lack of funds, because the Government—loved by the Powers on account of its weakness—has to part with all its funds to the military chieftains who fight each other and plunder the country, as in Europe—for China must be compared with Europe, not with any one of the petty States into which Europe is unhappily divided.

The students are not only full of public spirit themselves, but are a powerful force in arousing it throughout the nation. What they did in 1919, when Versailles awarded Shangtung to Japan, is well told by

Mr. Tyau in his chapter on "The Student Movement." And what they did was not merely political. To quote Mr. Tyau (p. 146):—

> Having aroused the nation, prevented the signature of the Versailles Treaty and assisted the merchants to enforce the Japanese boycott, the students then directed their energies to the enlightenment of their less educated brothers and sisters. For instance, by issuing publications, by popular lectures showing them the real situation, internally as well as externally; but especially by establishing free schools and maintaining them out of their own funds. No praise can be too high for such self-sacrifice, for the students generally also teach in these schools. The scheme is endorsed everywhere with the greatest enthusiasm, and in Peking alone it is estimated that fifty thousand children are benefited by such education.

One thing which came as a surprise to me was to find that, as regards modern education under Chinese control, there is complete equality between men and women. The position of women in Peking Government University is better than at Cambridge. Women are admitted to examinations and degrees, and there are women teachers in the university. The Girls' Higher Normal School in Peking, where prospective women teachers are taught, is a most excellent and progressive institution, and the spirit of free inquiry among the girls would horrify most British head mistresses.

There is a movement in favour of co-education, especially in elementary education, because, owing to the inadequate supply of schools, the girls tend to be left out altogether unless they can go to the same school as the boys. The first time I met Professor and Mrs. Dewey was at a banquet in Chang-sha, given by the Tuchun. When the time came for after-dinner speeches, Mrs. Dewey told the Tuchun that his province must adopt co-education. He made a statesmanlike reply, saying that the matter should receive his best consideration, but he feared the time was not ripe in Hunan. However, it was clear that the matter was within the sphere of practical politics. At the time, being new to China and having imagined China a somewhat backward country, I was surprised. Later on I realized that reforms which we only talk about can be actually carried out in China.

Education controlled by missionaries or conservative white men cannot give what Young China needs. After throwing off the native superstitions of centuries, it would be a dismal fiasco to take on the European superstitions which have been discarded here by all progressive people. It is only where progressive Chinese themselves are in control that there is scope for the renaissance spirit of the younger students, and for that free spirit of skeptical inquiry by which they are seeking to build a new civilization as splendid as their old civilization in its best days.

While I was in Peking, the Government teachers struck, not for higher pay, but for pay, because their salaries had not been paid for many months. Accompanied by some of the students, they went on a deputation to the Government, but were repulsed by soldiers and policemen, who clubbed them so severely that many had to be taken to hospital. The incident produced such universal fury that there was nearly a revolution, and the Government hastened to come to terms with the teachers with all possible speed. The modern teachers have behind them all that is virile, energetic, and public-spirited in China; the gang of bandits which controls the Government has behind it Japanese money and European intrigue. America occupies an intermediate position. One may say broadly that the old traditional education, with the military governors and the British and Japanese influence, stands for Conservatism; America and its commerce and its educational institutions stand for Liberalism; while the native modern education, practically though not theoretically, stands for Socialism. Incidentally, it alone stands for intellectual freedom.

The Chinese are a great nation, incapable of permanent suppression by foreigners. They will not consent to adopt our vices in order to acquire military strength; but they are willing to adopt our virtues in order to advance in wisdom. I think they are the only people in the world who quite genuinely believe that wisdom is more precious than rabies. That is why the West regards them as uncivilized.

## NOTES

1    It should be said that one sees just as fine buildings in purely Chinese institutions, such as Peking Government University and Nanking Teachers' Training
College.

2    Mr. Tyau (op. cit. p. 27) quotes from *Who's Who of American Returned Students,* a classification of the occupations of 596 Chinese who have returned
from American universities. The larger items are: In education, 38 as administrators and 197 as teachers; in Government service, 129 in executive offices
(there are also three members of Parliament and four judges); 95 engineers;
35 medical practitioners (including dentists); 60 in business; and 21 social
and religious workers. It is estimated that the total number of Chinese holding university degrees in America is 1,700, and in Great Britain 400 *(ib.).* This
disproportion is due to the more liberal policy of America in the matter of the
Boxer indemnity. In 1916 there were 292 Chinese university students in Great
Britain, and Mr. Tyau (p. 28) gives a classification of them by their subjects.
The larger groups are: Medicine, 50; law and economics, 47; engineering, 42;
mining, 22; natural science (including chemistry and geology, which are clas-
sified separately), 19.

# 14

## INDUSTRIALISM IN CHINA

China is as yet only slightly industrialized, but the industrial possibilities of the country are very great, and it may be taken as nearly certain that there will be a rapid development throughout the next few decades. China's future depends as much upon the manner of this development as upon any other single factor; and China's difficulties are very largely connected with the present industrial situation. I will therefore first briefly describe this situation, and then consider the possibilities of the near future.

We may take railways and mines as the foundation of a nation's industrial life. Let us therefore consider first the railways and then the mines, before going on to other matters.

When railways were new, the Manchu Government, like the universities of Oxford and Cambridge (which it resembled in many ways), objected to them, and did all it could to keep them at a distance.[1] In 1875 a short line was built by foreigners from Shanghai to Woosung, but the Central Government was so shocked that it caused it to be destroyed. In 1881 the first permanent railway was constructed, but not very much was accomplished until after the Japanese War of 1894–5. The Powers then thought that China was breaking up, and entered upon a scramble for concessions and spheres of influence. The Belgians built the important line from Peking to Hankow; the Americans obtained a concession for a Hankow-Canton railway, which, however, has only been constructed as far as Changsha. Russia built the Manchurian Railway, connecting Peking with the Siberian Railway and with Europe. Germany built the Shantung Railway, from Tsingtau to Tsinanfu. The French built a railway in the south. England sought to obtain a monopoly of the railways in the Yangtze valley. All these railways were to be owned by foreigners and managed by foreign officials of the respective countries which had obtained the concessions. The Boxer rising, however, made Europe aware that some caution was needed if the Chinese were not to be exasperated beyond endurance. After this, ownership of new railways was left to the Chinese Government, but with so much foreign control as to rob it of most of its value. By this time, Chinese public opinion had come to realize that there must be railways in China, and that the real problem was how to keep them under Chinese control. In 1908, the Tientsin-Pukow line and the Shanghai-Hangchow line were sanctioned, to be built by the help of foreign loans, but with all the administrative control in the hands of the Chinese Government. At the same time, the Peking-Hankow line was bought back by the Government, and the Peking-Kalgan line was constructed by the Chinese without foreign financial assistance. Of the big main lines of China, this left not much foreign control outside the Manchurian Railway (Chinese Eastern Railway) and the Shantung Railway. The first of these is mainly under foreign control and must now be regarded as permanently lost, until such time as China becomes strong enough to defeat Japan in war; and the whole of Manchuria has come more or less under Japanese control. But the Shantung Railway, by the agreement reached at Washington, is to be bought back by China—five years hence, if all goes well. Thus, except in regions practically lost to China, the Chinese now have control of all their more important railways, or will have before long. This is a very hopeful feature of the situation, and a distinct credit to Chinese sagacity.

Putnam Weale (Mr. Lennox Simpson) strongly urges—quite rightly, as I think—the great importance of nationalizing *all* Chinese railways. At Washington recently, he helped to secure the Shantung Railway award, and to concentrate attention on the railway as the main issue. Writing early in 1919, he said[2]:—

*The key to the proper control of China and the building-up of the new Republican State is the railway key.* . . . The revolution of 1911, and the acceptance in principle of Western ideas of popular government, removed the danger of foreign provinces being carved out of the old Manchu Empire. There was, however, left behind a more subtle weapon. *This weapon is the railway.* Russia with her Manchurian Railway scheme taught Japan the new method. Japan, by the Treaty of Portsmouth in 1905, not only inherited the richer half of the Manchurian railways, but was able to put into practice a new technique, based on a mixture of twisted economics, police control, and military garrisons. Out of this grew the latter-day highly developed railway-zone which, to all intents and purposes, creates a new type of foreign *enclave*, subversive of the Chinese State. *The especial evil to-day is that Japan has transferred from Manchuria to Shantung this new technique*, which . . . she will eventually extend into the very heart of intramural China . . . and also into extramural Chihli and Inner Mongolia (thus outflanking Peking) unless she is summarily arrested. *At all costs this must be stopped.* The method of doing so is easy: *It is to have it laid down categorically, and accepted by all the Powers, that henceforth all railways on Chinese soil are a vital portion of Chinese sovereignty and must be controlled directly from Peking by a National Railway Board; that stationmasters, personnel and police, must be Chinese citizens, technical foreign help being limited to a set standard; and that all railway concessions are henceforth to be considered simply as building concessions which must be handed over, section by section, as they are built, to the National Railway Board.*

If the Shantung Railway Agreement is loyally carried out, this reform—as to whose importance I quite agree with Putnam Weale—will have been practically completed five years hence. But we must expect Japan to adopt every possible means of avoiding the carrying out of her promises, from instigating Chinese civil war to the murdering of Japanese employees by Japanese secret agents masquerading as Chinese. Therefore, until the Chinese actually have complete control of the Shantung Railway, we cannot feel confident that they will ever get it.

It must not be supposed that the Chinese run railways badly. The Kalgan Railway, which they built, is just as well built as those constructed by foreigners; and the lines under Chinese administration are admirably managed. I quote from Mr. Tyau[3] the following statistics, which refer to the year 1919: Government railways, in operation, 6027 kilometres; under construction, 383 kilometres; private and provincial railways, 773 kilometres; concessioned railways, 3,780 kilometres. Total, 10,963 kilometres, or 6,852 miles. (The concessioned railways are mainly those in Manchuria and Shantung, of which the first must be regarded as definitely lost to China, while the second is probably recovered. The problem of concessioned railways has therefore no longer the importance that it had, though, by detaching Manchuria, the foreign railway has shown its power for evil). As regards financial results, Mr. Tyau gives the following figures for the principal State railways in 1918:—

| Name of Line | Kilometres operated | Year completed | Per cent earned on investment |
|---|---|---|---|
| Peking-Mukden | 987 | 1897 | 22·7 |
| Peking-Hankow | 1306 | 1905 | 15·8 |
| Shanghai-Nanking | 327 | 1908 | 6·2 |
| Tientsin-Pukow | 1107 | 1912 | 6·2 |
| Peking-Suiyuan | 490 | 1915 | 5·6 |

Subsequent years, for which I have not the exact figures, have been less prosperous.

I cannot discover any evidence of incompetence in Chinese railway administration. On the contrary, much has been done to overcome the evils due to the fact that the various lines were originally constructed by different Powers, each following its own customs, so that there was no uniformity, and goods trucks could not be moved from one line on to another. There is, however, urgent need of further railways, especially to open up the west and to connect Canton with Hankow, the profit of which would probably be enormous.

Mines are perhaps as important as railways, for if a country allows foreign control of its mineral resources it cannot build up either its industries or its munitions to the point where they will be independent of foreign favour. But the situation as regards mining is at present far from satisfactory.

Mr. Julean Arnold, American Commercial Attaché at Peking, writing early in 1919, made the following statement as regards China's mineral resources:—

China is favoured with a wonderful wealth in coal and in a good supply of iron ore, two essentials to modern industrial development. To indicate how little China has developed its marvellous wealth in coal, this country imported, during 1917, 14,000,000 tons. It is estimated that China produces now 20,000,000 tons annually, but it is supposed to have richer resources in coal than has the United States which, in 1918, produced 650,000,000 tons. In iron ore it has been estimated that China has 400,000,000 tons suitable for furnace reaction, and an additional 300,000,000 tons which might be worked by native methods. During 1917, it is estimated that China's production of pig iron was 500,000 tons. The developments in the iron and steel industry in China are making rapid strides, and a few years hence it is expected that the production of pig iron and of finished steel will be several millions of tons annually. . . . In antimony and tin China is also particularly rich, and considerable progress has taken place in the mining and smelting of these ores during the past few years. China should jealously safeguard its mineral wealth, so as to preserve it for the country's welfare.[4]

The China Year Book for 1919 gives the total Chinese production of coal for 1914 as 6,316,735 tons, and of iron ore at 468,938 tons.[5] Comparing these with Mr. Arnold's figures for 1917, namely 20,000,000 tons of coal and 500,000 tons of pig iron (not iron ore), it is evident that great progress was made during those three years, and there is every reason to think that at least the same rate of progress has been maintained. The main problem for China, however, is not *rapid* development, but *national* development. Japan is poor in minerals, and has set to work to acquire as much as possible of the mineral wealth of China. This is important to Japan, for two different reasons: first, that only industrial development can support the growing population, which cannot be induced to emigrate to Japanese possessions on the mainland; secondly, that steel is an indispensable requisite for imperialism.

The Chinese are proud of the Kiangnan dock and engineering works at Shanghai, which is a Government concern, and has proved its capacity for shipbuilding on modern lines. It built four ships of 10,000 tons each for the American Government. Mr. S. G. Cheng[6] says: —

> For the construction of these ships, materials were mostly supplied by China, except steel, which had to be shipped from America and Europe (the steel produced in China being so limited in quantity, that after a certain amount is exported to Japan by virtue of a previous contract, little is left for home consumption).

Considering how rich China is in iron ore, this state of affairs needs explanation. The explanation is valuable to anyone who wishes to understand modern politics.

The China Year Book for 1919[7] (a work as little concerned with politics as Whitaker's Almanack) gives a list of the five principal iron mines in China, with some information about each. The first and most important are the Tayeh mines, worked by the Hanyehping Iron and Coal Co., Ltd., which, as the reader may remember, was the subject of the third group in the Twenty-one Demands. The total amount of ore in sight is estimated by the China Year Book at 50,000,000 tons, derived chiefly from two mines, in one of which the ore yields 65 per cent of iron, in the other 58 to 63 per cent. The output for 1916 is given as 603,732 tons (it has been greatly increased since then). The Year Book proceeds: "Japanese capital is invested in the Company, and by the agreement between China and Japan of May 1915 [after the ultimatum which enforced the revised Twenty-one Demands], the Chinese Government undertook not to convert the Company into a State-owned concern nor to compel it to borrow money from other than Japanese sources." It should be added that there is a Japanese accountant and a Japanese technical adviser, and that pig-iron and ore, up to a specified value, must be sold to the Imperial Japanese works at much below the market price, leaving a paltry residue for sale in the open market.[8]

The second item in the China Year Book's list is the Tungkuan Shan mines. All that is said about these is as follows: "Tungling district on the Yangtze, 55 miles above Wuhu, Anhui province. A concession to work these mines, granted to the London and China Syndicate (British) in 1904, was surrendered in 1910 for the sum of £52,000, and the mines were transferred to a Chinese Company to be formed for their exploitation." These mines, therefore, are in Chinese hands. I do not know what their capacity is supposed to be, and in view of the price at which they were sold, it cannot be very great. The capital of the Hanyehping Co. is $20,000,000, which is considerably more than £52,000. This was the only one of the five iron mines mentioned in the Year Book which was not in Japanese hands at the time when the Year Book was published.

Next comes the Taochung Iron Mine, Anhui province. "The concession which was granted to the Sino-Japanese Industrial Development Co. will be worked by the Orient Steel Manufacturing Co. The mine is said to contain 60,000,000 tons of ore, containing 65 per cent of pure iron. The plan of operations provides for the production of pig iron at the rate of 170,000 tons a year, a steel mill with a capacity of 100,000 tons of steel ingots a year, and a casting and forging mill to produce 75,000 tons a year."

The fourth mine is at Chinlingchen, in Shantung, "worked in conjunction with the Hengshan Colliery by the railway." I presume it is to be sold back to China along with the railway.

The fifth and last mine mentioned is the Penhsihu Mine, "one of the most promising mines in the nine mining areas in South Manchuria, where the Japanese are permitted by an exchange of Notes between the Chinese and Japanese Governments (May 25, 1915) to prospect for and operate mines. The seam of this mine extends from near Liaoyang to the neighbourhood of Penhsihu, and in size is pronounced equal to the Tayeh mine." It will be observed that this mine, also, was acquired by the Japanese as a result of the ultimatum enforcing the Twenty-one Demands. The *Year Book* adds: "The Japanese Navy is purchasing some of the Penhsihu output. Osaka ironworks placed an order for 15,000 tons in 1915 and the arsenal at Osaka in the same year accepted a tender for Penhsihu iron."

It will be seen from these facts that, as regards iron, the Chinese have allowed the Japanese to acquire a position of vantage from which they can only be ousted with great difficulty. Nevertheless, it is absolutely imperative that the Chinese should develop an iron and steel industry of their own on a large scale. If they do not, they cannot preserve their national independence, their own civilization, or any of the things that make them potentially of value to the world. It should be observed that the chief reason for which the Japanese desire Chinese iron is in order to be able to exploit and tyrannize over China. Confucius, I understand, says nothing about iron mines;[9] therefore the old-fashioned Chinese did not realize the importance of preserving them. Now that they are awake to the situation, it is almost too late. I shall come back later to the question of what can be done. For the present, let us continue our survey of facts.

It may be presumed that the population of China will always be mainly agricultural. Tea, silk, raw cotton, grain, the soya bean, etc., are crops in which China excels. In production of raw cotton, China is the third country in the world, India being the first and the United States the second. There is, of course, room for great progress in agriculture, but industry is vital if China is to preserve her national independence, and it is industry that is our present topic.

To quote Mr. Tyau: "At the end of 1916 the number of factory hands was officially estimated at 560,000 and that of mine workers 406,000. Since then no official returns for the whole country have been published . . . but perhaps a million each would be an approximate figure for the present number of factory operatives and mine workers."[10] Of course, the hours are very long and the wages very low; Mr. Tyau mentions as specially modern and praiseworthy certain textile factories where the wages range from 15 to 45 cents a day.[11] (The cent varies in value, but is always somewhere between a farthing and a halfpenny.) No doubt as industry develops Socialism and labour unrest will also develop. If Mr. Tyau is to be taken as a sample of the modern Chinese governing classes, the policy of the Government towards Labour will be very illiberal. Mr. Tyau's outlook is that of an American capitalist, and shows the extent to which he has come under American influence, as well as that of conservative England (he is an LL.D. of London). Most of the Young Chinese I came across, however, were Socialists, and it may be hoped that the traditional Chinese dislike of uncompromising fierceness will make the Government less savage against Labour than the Governments of America and Japan.

There is room for the development of a great textile industry in China. There are a certain number of modern mills, and nothing but enterprise is needed to make the industry as great as that of Lancashire.

Shipbuilding has made a good beginning in Shanghai, and would probably develop rapidly if China had a flourishing iron and steel industry in native hands.

The total exports of native produce in 1919 were just under £200,000,000 (630,000,000 taels), and the total imports slightly larger. It is better, however, to consider such statistics in taels, because currency fluctuations make the results deceptive when reckoned in sterling. The tael is not a coin, but a certain weight of silver, and therefore its value fluctuates with the value of silver. The China Year Book gives imports and exports of Chinese produce for 1902 as 325 million taels and 214 million taels respectively; for 1911, as 482 and 377; for 1917, as 577 and 462; for 1920, as 762 and 541. (The corresponding figures in pounds sterling for 1911 are 64 millions and 50 millions; for 1917, 124 millions and 99,900,000.) It will thus be seen that, although the foreign trade of China is still small in proportion to population, it is increasing very fast. To a European it is always surprising to find how little the economic life of China is affected by such incidents as revolutions and civil wars.

Certain principles seem to emerge from a study of the Chinese railways and mines as needing to be adopted by the Chinese Government if national independence is to be preserved. As regards railways, nationalization is obviously desirable, even if it somewhat retards the building of new lines. Railways not in the hands of the Government will be controlled, in the end if not in the beginning, by foreigners, who will thus acquire a power over China which will be fatal to freedom. I think we may hope that the Chinese authorities now realize this, and will henceforth act upon it.

In regard to mines, development by the Chinese themselves is urgent, since undeveloped resources tempt the greed of the Great Powers, and development by foreigners makes it possible to keep China enslaved. It should therefore be enacted that, in future, no sale of mines or of any interest in mines to foreigners, and no loan from foreigners on the security of mines, will be recognized as legally valid. In view of extra-territoriality, it will be difficult to induce foreigners to accept such legislation, and Consular Courts will not readily admit its validity. But, as the example of extra-territoriality in Japan shows, such matters depend upon the national strength; if the Powers fear China, they will recognize the validity of Chinese legislation, but if not, not. In view of the need of rapid development of mining by Chinese, it would probably be unwise to nationalize all mines here and now. It would be better to provide every possible encouragement to genuinely Chinese private enterprise, and to offer the assistance of geological and mining experts, etc. The Government should, however, retain the right (a) to buy out any mining concern at a fair valuation;

(6) to work minerals itself in cases where the private owners fail to do so, in spite of expert opinion in favour of their being worked. These powers should be widely exercised, and as soon as mining has reached the point compatible with national security, the mines should be all nationalized, except where, as at Tayeh, diplomatic agreements stand in the way. It is clear that the Tayeh mines must be recovered by China as soon as opportunity offers, but when or how that will be it is as yet impossible to say. Of course I have been assuming an orderly government established in China, but without that nothing vigorous can be done to repel foreign aggression. This is a point to which, along with other general questions connected with the industrializing of China, I shall return in my last chapter.

It is said by Europeans who have business experience in China that the Chinese are not good at managing large joint-stock companies, such as modern industry requires. As everyone knows, they are proverbially honest in business, in spite of the corruption of their politics. But their successful businesses—so one gathers—do not usually extend beyond a single family; and even they are apt to come to grief sooner or later through nepotism. This is what Europeans say; I cannot speak from my own knowledge. But I am convinced that modern education is very quickly changing this state of affairs, which was connected with Confucianism and the family ethic. Many Chinese have been trained in business methods in America; there are Colleges of Commerce at Woosung and other places; and the patriotism of Young China has led men of the highest education to devote themselves to industrial development. The Chinese are no doubt, by temperament and tradition, more suited to commerce than to industry, but contact with the West is rapidly introducing new aptitudes and a new mentality. There is, therefore, every reason to expect, if political conditions are not too adverse, that the industrial development of China will proceed rapidly throughout the next few decades. It is of vital importance that that development should be controlled by the Chinese rather than by foreign nations. But that is part of the larger problem of the recovery of Chinese independence, with which I shall deal in my last chapter.

## NOTES

1 For the history of Chinese railways, see Tyau, op. cit. pp. 183 ff.
2 *China in 1918*. Published by the *Peking Leader*, pp. 45–6.
3 Op. cit. chap. xi.
4 *China in 1918*, p. 26. There is perhaps some mistake in the figures given for iron ore, as the Tayeh mines alone are estimated by some to contain 700,000,000 tons of iron ore. Coleman, op. cit. p. 51.
5 Page 63. The 1922 *Year Book* gives 19,500,000 tons of coal production.
6 *Modern China*, p. 265.
7 Pages 74–5.
8 Coleman, op, cit. chap. xiv.
9 It seems it would be inaccurate to maintain that there is nothing on the subject in the Gospels. An eminent American divine pointed out in print, as regards the advice against laying up treasure where moth and rust doth corrupt, that "moth and rust do not get at Mr. Rockefeller's oil wells, and thieves do not often break through and steal a railway. What Jesus condemned was hoarding wealth." See Upton Sinclair, *The Profits of Religion,* 1918, p. 175.
10 Page 237.
11 Page 218.

# 15

## THE OUTLOOK FOR CHINA

In this chapter I propose to take, as far as I am able, the standpoint of a progressive and public-spirited Chinese, and consider what reforms, in what order, I should advocate in that case.

To begin with, it is clear that China must be saved by her own efforts, and cannot rely upon outside help. In the international situation, China has had both good and bad fortune. The Great War was unfortunate, because it gave Japan temporarily a free hand; the collapse of Tsarist Russia was fortunate, because it put an end to the secret alliance of Russians and Japanese; the Anglo-Japanese Alliance was unfortunate, because it compelled us to abet Japanese aggression even against our own economic interests; the friction between Japan and America was fortunate; but the agreement arrived at by the Washington Conference, though momentarily advantageous as regards Shantung, is likely, in the long run, to prove unfortunate, since it will make America less willing to oppose Japan. For reasons which I set forth in Chap. X., unless China becomes strong, either the collapse of Japan or her unquestioned ascendency in the Far East is almost certain to prove disastrous to China; and one or other of these is very likely to come about. All the Great Powers, without exception, have interests which are incompatible, in the long run, with China's welfare and with the best development of Chinese civilization. Therefore the Chinese must seek salvation in their own energy, not in the benevolence of any outside Power.

The problem is not merely one of *political* independence; a certain cultural independence is at least as important. I have tried to show in this book that the Chinese are, in certain ways, superior to us, and it would not be good either for them or for us if, in these ways, they had to descend to our level in order to preserve their existence as a nation. In this matter, however, a compromise is necessary. Unless they adopt some of our vices to some extent, we shall not respect them, and they will be increasingly oppressed by foreign nations. The object must be to keep this process within the narrowest limits compatible with safety.

First of all, a patriotic spirit is necessary—not, of course, the bigoted anti-foreign spirit of the Boxers, but the enlightened attitude which is willing to learn from other nations while not willing to allow them to dominate. This attitude has been generated among educated Chinese, and to a great extent in the merchant class, by the brutal tuition of Japan. The danger of patriotism is that, as soon as it has proved strong enough for successful defence, it is apt to turn to foreign aggression. China, by her resources and her population, is capable of being the greatest Power in the world after the United States. It is much to be feared that, in the process of becoming strong enough to preserve their independence, the Chinese may become strong enough to embark upon a career of imperialism. It cannot be too strongly urged that patriotism should be only defensive, not aggressive. But with this proviso, I think a spirit of patriotism is absolutely necessary to the regeneration of China. Independence is to be sought, not as an end in itself, but as a means towards a new blend of Western skill with the traditional Chinese virtues. If this end is not achieved, political independence will have little value.

The three chief requisites, I should say, are: (1) The establishment of an orderly Government; (2) industrial development under Chinese control; (3) The spread of education. All these aims will have to be pursued concurrently, but on the whole their urgency seems to me to come in the above order. We have already seen how large a part the State will have to take in building up industry, and how impossible this is while the political anarchy continues. Funds for education on a large scale are also unobtainable until there is good government. Therefore good government is the prerequisite of all other reforms. Industrialism and education are closely connected, and it would be difficult to decide the priority between them; but I have put industrialism first, because, unless it is developed very soon by the Chinese, foreigners will have acquired such a strong hold that it will be very difficult indeed to oust them. These reasons have decided me that our three problems ought to be taken in the above order.

1. *The establishment of an orderly government.*—At the moment of writing, the condition of China is as anarchic as it has ever been. A battle between Chang-tso-lin and Wu-Pei-Fu is imminent; the former is usually considered, though falsely according to some good authorities, the most reactionary force in China; Wu-Pei-Fu, though *The Times* calls him "the Liberal leader," may well prove no more satisfactory than "Liberal" leaders nearer home. It is of course possible that, if he wins, he may be true to his promises and convoke a Parliament for all China; but it is at least equally possible that he may not. In any case, to depend upon the favour of a successful general is as precarious as to depend upon the benevolence of a foreign Power. If the progressive elements are to win, they must become a strong organized force.

So far as I can discover, Chinese Constitutionalists are doing the best thing that is possible at the moment, namely, concerting a joint programme, involving the convoking of a Parliament and the cessation of military usurpation. Union is essential, even if it involves sacrifice of cherished beliefs on the part of some. Given a programme upon which all the Constitutionalists are united, they will acquire great weight in public opinion, which is very powerful in China. They may then be able, sooner or later, to offer a high constitutional position to some powerful general, on condition of his ceasing to depend upon mere military force. By this means they may be able to turn the scales in favour of the man they select, as the student agitation turned the scales in July 1920 in favour of Wu-Pei-Fu against the An Fu party. Such a policy can only be successful if it is combined with vigorous propaganda, both among the civilian population and among the soldiers, and if, as soon as peace is restored, work is found for disbanded soldiers and pay for those who are not disbanded. This raises the financial problem, which is very difficult, because foreign Powers will not lend except in return for some further sacrifice of the remnants of Chinese independence. (For reasons explained in Chap. X., I do not accept the statement by the American consortium bankers that a loan from them would not involve control over China's internal affairs. They may not mean control to be involved, but I am convinced that in fact it would be.) The only way out of this difficulty that I can see is to raise an internal loan by appealing to the patriotism of Chinese merchants. There is plenty of money in China, but, very naturally, rich Chinese will not lend to any of the brigands who now control the Government.

When the time comes to draft a permanent Constitution, I have no doubt that it will have to be federal, allowing a very large measure of autonomy to the provinces, and reserving for the Central Government few things except customs, army and navy, foreign relations and railways. Provincial feeling is strong, and it is now, I think, generally recognized that a mistake was made in 1912 in not allowing it more scope.

While a Constitution is being drafted, and even after it has been agreed upon, it will not be possible to rely upon the inherent prestige of Constitutionalism, or to leave public opinion without guidance. It will be necessary for the genuinely progressive people throughout the country to unite in a strongly disciplined society, arriving at collective decisions and enforcing support of those decisions upon all its members. This society will have to win the confidence of public opinion by a very rigid avoidance of corruption and political profiteering; the slightest failure of a member in this respect must be visited by expulsion. The society must make itself obviously the champion of the national interests as against all self-seekers, speculators and toadies to foreign Powers. It will thus become able authoritatively to commend or condemn politicians and to wield great influence over opinion, even in the army. There exists in Young China enough energy, patriotism and honesty to create such a society and to make it strong through the respect which it will command. But unless enlightened patriotism is organized in some such way, its power will not be equal to the political problems with which China is faced.

Sooner or later, the encroachments of foreign Powers upon the sovereign rights of China must be swept away. The Chinese must recover the Treaty Ports, control of the tariff, and so on; they must also free themselves from extra-territoriality. But all this can probably be done, as it was in Japan, without offending foreign Powers (except perhaps the Japanese). It would be a mistake to complicate the early stages of Chinese recovery by measures which would antagonize foreign Powers in general. Russia was in a stronger position for defence than China, yet Russia has suffered terribly from the universal hostility provoked by the Bolsheviks. Given good government and a development of China's resources, it will be possible to obtain most of the needed concessions by purely diplomatic means; the rest can wait for a suitable opportunity.

2. *Industrial development.*—On this subject I have already written in Chap. XIV.; it is certain general aspects of the subject that I wish to consider now. For reasons already given, I hold that all railways ought to be in the hands of the State, and that all successful mines ought to be purchased by the State at a fair valuation, even if they are not State-owned from the first. Contracts with foreigners for loans ought to be carefully drawn so as to leave the control to China. There would not be much difficulty about this if China had a stable and orderly government; in that case, many foreign capitalists would be willing to lend on good security, without exacting any part in the management. Every possible diplomatic method should be employed to break down such a monopoly as the consortium seeks to acquire in the matter of loans.

Given good government, a large amount of State enterprise would be desirable in Chinese industry. There are many arguments for State Socialism, or rather what Lenin calls State Capitalism, in any country which is economically but not culturally backward. In the first place, it is easier for the State to borrow than for a private person; in the second place, it is easier for the State to engage and employ the foreign experts who are likely to be needed for some time to come; in the third place, it is easier for the State to make sure that vital industries do not come under the control of foreign Powers. What is perhaps more important than any of these considerations is that, by undertaking industrial enterprise from the first, the State can prevent the growth of many of the evils of private capitalism. If China can acquire a vigorous and honest State, it will be possible to develop Chinese industry without, at the same time, developing the overweening power of private capitalists by which the Western nations are now both oppressed and misled.

But if this is to be done successfully, it will require a great change in Chinese morals, a development of public spirit in place of the family ethic, a transference to the public service of that honesty which already exists in private business, and a degree of energy which is at present rare. I believe that Young China is capable of fulfilling these requisites, spurred on by patriotism; but it is important to realize that they are requisites, and that, without them, any system of State Socialism must fail.

For industrial development, it is important that the Chinese should learn to become technical experts and also to become skilled workers. I think more has been done towards the former of these needs than towards the latter. For the latter purpose, it would probably be wise to import skilled workmen—say from Germany—and cause them to give instruction to Chinese workmen in any new branch of industrial work that it might be desired to develop.

3. *Education.*—If China is to become a democracy, as most progressive Chinese hope, universal education is imperative. Where the bulk of the population cannot read, true democracy is impossible. Education is a good in itself, but is also essential for developing political

consciousness, of which at present there is almost none in rural China. The Chinese themselves are well aware of this, but in the present state of the finances it is impossible to establish universal elementary education. Until it has been established for some time, China must be, in fact, if not in form, an oligarchy, because the uneducated masses cannot have any effective political opinion. Even given good government, it is doubtful whether the immense expense of educating such a vast population could be borne by the nation without a considerable industrial development. Such industrial development as already exists is mainly in the hands of foreigners, and its profits provide warships for the Japanese, or mansions and dinners for British and American millionaires. If its profits are to provide the funds for Chinese education, industry must be in Chinese hands. This is another reason why industrial development must probably precede any complete scheme of education.

For the present, even if the funds existed, there would not be sufficient teachers to provide a schoolmaster in every village. There is, however, such an enthusiasm for education in China that teachers are being trained as fast as is possible with such limited resources; indeed a great deal of devotion and public spirit is being shown by Chinese educators, whose salaries are usually many months in arrears.

Chinese control is, to my mind, as important in the matter of education as in the matter of industry. For the present, it is still necessary to have foreign instructors in some subjects, though this necessity will soon cease. Foreign instructors, however, provided they are not too numerous, do no harm, any more than foreign experts in railways and mines. What does harm is foreign management. Chinese educated in mission schools, or in lay establishments controlled by foreigners, tend to become de-nationalized, and to have a slavish attitude towards Western civilization. This unfits them for taking a useful part in the national life, and tends to undermine their morals. Also, oddly enough, it makes them more conservative in purely Chinese matters than the young men and women who have had a modern education under Chinese auspices. Europeans in general are more conservative about China than the modern Chinese are, and they tend to convey their conservatism to their pupils. And of course their whole influence, unavoidably if involuntarily, militates against national self-respect in those whom they teach.

Those who desire to do research in some academic subject will, for some time to come, need a period of residence in some European or American university. But for the great majority of university students it is far better, if possible, to acquire their education in China. Returned students have, to a remarkable extent, the stamp of the country from which they have returned, particularly when that country is America. A society such as was foreshadowed earlier in this chapter, in which all really progressive Chinese should combine, would encounter difficulties, as things stand, from the divergencies in national bias between students returned from (say) Japan, America and Germany. Given time, this difficulty can be overcome by the increase in purely Chinese university education, but at present the difficulty would be serious.

To overcome this difficulty, two things are needed: inspiring leadership, and a clear conception of the kind of civilization to be aimed at. Leadership will have to be both intellectual and practical. As regards intellectual leadership, China is a country where writers have enormous influence, and a vigorous reformer possessed of literary skill could carry with him the great majority of Young China. Men with the requisite gifts exist in China; I might mention, as an example personally known to me, Dr. Hu Suh.[1] He has great learning, wide culture, remarkable energy, and a fearless passion for reform; his writings in the vernacular inspire enthusiasm among progressive Chinese. He is in favour of assimilating all that is good in Western culture, but by no means a slavish admirer of our ways.

The practical political leadership of such a society as I conceive to be needed would probably demand different gifts from those required in an intellectual leader. It is therefore likely that the two could not be combined in one man, but would need men as different as Lenin and Karl Marx.

The aim to be pursued is of importance, not only to China, but to the world. Out of the renaissance spirit now existing in China, it is possible, if foreign nations can be prevented from working havoc, to develop a new civilization better than any that the world has yet known. This is the aim which Young China should set before itself: the preservation of the urbanity and courtesy, the candour and the pacific temper, which are characteristic of the Chinese nation, together with a knowledge of Western science and an application of it to the practical problems of China. Of such practical problems there are two kinds: one due to the internal condition of China, and the other to its international situation. In the former class come education, democracy, the diminution of poverty, hygiene and sanitation, and the prevention of famines. In the latter class come the establishment of a strong government, the development of industrialism, the revision of treaties and the recovery of the Treaty Ports (as to which Japan may serve as a model), and finally, the creation of an army sufficiently strong to defend the country against Japan. Both classes of problems demand Western science. But they do not demand the adoption of the Western philosophy of life.

If the Chinese were to adopt the Western philosophy of life, they would, as soon as they had made themselves safe against foreign aggression, embark upon aggression on their own account. They would repeat the campaigns of the Han and Tang dynasties in Central Asia, and perhaps emulate Kublai by the invasion of Japan. They would exploit their material resources with a view to producing a few bloated plutocrats at home and millions dying of hunger abroad. Such are the results which the West achieves by the application of science. If China were led astray by the lure of brutal power, she might repel her enemies outwardly, but would have yielded to them inwardly. It is not unlikely that the great military nations of the modern world will bring about their own destruction by their inability to abstain from war, which will become, with every year that passes, more scientific and more devastating. If China joins in this madness, China will perish like the rest. But if Chinese reformers can have the moderation to stop when they have made China capable of self-defence, and to abstain from the further step of foreign conquest; if, when they have become safe at home, they can turn aside from the materialistic activities imposed by the Powers, and devote their freedom to science and art and the inauguration of a better economic system—then China will have played the part in the world for which she is fitted, and will have given to mankind as a whole new hope in the moment of greatest need. It is this hope that I wish to see inspiring Young China. This hope is realizable; and because it is realizable, China deserves a foremost place in the esteem of every lover of mankind.

## NOTE

1    An account of a portion of his work will be found in Tyau, op. cit. pp. 40 ff.

# APPENDIX

While the above pages were going through the Press, some important developments have taken place in China. Wu-Pei-Fu has defeated Chang-tso-lin and made himself master of Peking. Chang has retreated towards Manchuria with a broken army, and proclaimed the independence of Manchuria. This might suit the Japanese very well, but it is hardly to be supposed that the other Powers would acquiesce. It is, therefore, not unlikely that Chang may lose Manchuria also, and cease to be a factor in Chinese politics.

For the moment, Wu-Pei-Fu controls the greater part of China, and his intentions become important. The British in China have, for some years, befriended him, and this fact colours all Press telegrams appearing in our newspapers. According to *The Times*, he has pronounced in favour of the reassembling of the old all-China Parliament, with a view to the restoration of constitutional government. This is a measure in which the South could concur, and if he really adheres to this intention he has it in his power to put an end to Chinese anarchy. *The Times* Peking correspondent, telegraphing on May 30, reports that "Wu-Pei-Fu declares that if the old Parliament will reassemble and work in national interests he will support it up to the limit, and fight any obstructionists."

On May 18, the same correspondent telegraphed that "Wu-Pei-Fu is lending his support to the unification movements, and has found common ground for action with Chen Chiung Ming," who is Sun's colleague at Canton and is engaged in civil war with Sun, who is imperialistic and wants to conquer all China for his government, said to be alone constitutional. The programme agreed upon between Wu and Chen Chiung Ming is given in the same telegram as follows:

> Local self-government shall be established and magistrates shall be elected by the people; District police shall be created under District Boards subject to Central Provincial Boards; Civil governors shall be responsible to the Central Government, not to the Tuchuns; a national army shall be created, controlled and paid by the Central Government; Provincial police and *gendarmerie*, not the Tuchuns or the army, shall be responsible for peace and order in the provinces; the whole nation shall agree to recall the old Parliament and the restoration of the Provisional Constitution of the first year of the Republic; Taxes shall be collected by the Central Government, and only a stipulated sum shall be granted to each province for expenses, the balance to be forwarded to the Central Government as under the Ching dynasty; Afforestation shall be undertaken, industries established, highways built, and other measures taken to keep the people on the land.

This is an admirable programme, but it is impossible to know how much of it will ever be carried out.

Meanwhile, Sun Yat Sen is still at war with Wu-Pei-Fu. It has been stated in the British Press that there was an alliance between Sun and Chang, but it seems there was little more than a common hostility to Wu. Sun's friends maintain that he is a genuine Constitutionalist, and that Wu is not to be trusted, but Chen Chiung Ming has a better reputation than Sun among reformers. The British in China all praise Wu and hate Sun; the Americans all praise Sun and decry Wu. Sun undoubtedly has a past record of genuine patriotism, and there can be no doubt that the Canton Government has been the best in China. What appears in our newspapers on the subject is certainly designed to give a falsely unfavourable impression of Canton. For example, in *The Times* of May 15, a telegram appeared from Hong-Kong to the following effect:

> I learn that the troops of Sun Yat Sen, President of South China, which are stated to be marching north from Canton, are a rabble. Many are without weapons and a large percentage of the uniforms are merely rags. There is no discipline, and gambling and opium-smoking are rife.

Nevertheless, on May 30, *The Times* had to confess that this army had won a brilliant victory, capturing "the most important stronghold in Kiangsi," together with 40 field guns and large quantities of munitions.

The situation must remain obscure until more detailed news has arrived by mail. It is to be hoped that the Canton Government, through the victory of Chen Chiung Ming, will come to terms with Wu-Pei-Fu, and will be strong enough to compel him to adhere to the terms. It is to be hoped also that Chang's proclamation of the independence of Manchuria will not be seized upon by Japan as an excuse for a more complete absorption of that country. If Wu-Pei-Fu adheres to the declaration quoted above, there can be no patriotic reason why Canton should not co-operate with him; on the other hand, the military strength of Canton makes it more likely that Wu will find it prudent to adhere to his declaration. There is certainly a better chance than there was before the defeat of Chang for the unification of China and the ending of the Tuchuns' tyranny. But it is as yet no more than a chance, and the future is still problematical.

June 21, 1922

# Postscript

Since this book was written nothing decisive has happened in China, but certain developments, internal and external, deserve to be noted. There has been no visible approach towards stable government; in fact, on the surface, everything has tended in the opposite direction. But there has been an increase in the diffusion of intelligent patriotism, which, it may be hoped, will bear fruit in time.

Externally, the principal source of change has been the Washington Conference, whose effects were not yet visible when this book was written. By that conference Japan was deprived of the British Alliance, with the result that Japanese statesmen became more conciliatory in their dealings with China and Russia. They have evacuated Shantung and Vladivostok, and have become markedly less imperialistic than during the war. If I were writing now, I would speak less unfavourably of Japan, though I still consider Japan's behaviour to China from 1914 to 1921 deserves severe criticism. Since that date, however, pre-eminence in evildoing has passed from Japan to Great Britain. In the South, although Sun Yat Sen is dead, the character of the Canton Government remains progressive and patriotic; its relations to Hong Kong have been, for a long time, little short of war, and Hong Kong has been nearly ruined by the Cantonese boycott. After long refusal to negotiate, the British authorities have at last been compelled to recognize that they cannot defeat the boycott, and have therefore appointed an official delegation in the hope of establishing some *modus vivendi.*

In the North, events have centred round the curious career of Feng, the Christian General as he used to be called in the British Press, or the "Christian" General, as he became, when he turned anti-British. Originally a lieutenant of Wu-Pei-Fu, he occupied Peking, nominally in Wu's interests, during the annual clash between Wu and Chang. He thereupon suddenly abandoned Wu's cause, became an ardent nationalist, and turned to Russia for support. During the period of his ascendancy, nationalism made great strides in China. Partly from the nature of the case, partly under Russian guidance, the Nationalist movement has been predominantly anti-British. The English, finding themselves disliked, cast about for methods of acquiring popularity. They shot down a considerable number of unarmed students in Shanghai without giving them a chance to escape by first threatening to fire. In Shameen, the European quarter of Canton, a similar incident occurred; but in this case there is a conflict of testimony as to who fired the first shot. These measures, strange to say, did not succeed in inspiring the Chinese with any very ardent affection for us. For a time, it seemed as if nationalism, under Russian guidance, would succeed in making the position of the British in China impossible. But a momentary reconciliation was effected between Chang and Wu, the proteges of Japan and Great Britain respectively; and, by their alliance, they succeeded in driving the nationalist armies out of Peking into the northern hills, while Feng himself retired temporarily to Moscow.

Even now, however, the situation is not all that we could desire. It is clear that Chang and Wu must soon quarrel again, and the Nationalist armies are intact. The Tuchuns whom we befriended have, in some important places, seized the Salt Gabelle, to the great indignation of the bondholders. The students, under the guidance of all the most eminent intellectuals of China, have become bitterly hostile to all foreign Powers except Russia, and are liable to turn the scale, by propaganda among the soldiers, as they did in 1920. The Americans, alarmed by the Bolshevik bogey, are more and more inclined to take the British view of Chinese needs. The British view is still that China needs a central government strong enough to suppress internal anarchy, but weak enough to be always obliged to yield to foreign pressure. The Chinese themselves, under our tuition, have increasingly learnt the lesson which the Japanese began to teach them, namely, that their lives cannot be secure until they become a strong military power. As for the British, they have suffered appalling losses in trade, and they will in time lose everything, from their inability to respect the most elementary rights of the Chinese, which was displayed most dramatically in the Shanghai massacre.

An Act has been passed through the British Parliament to the effect that the residue of the Boxer Indemnity shall be spent, for the mutual benefit of China and Great Britain, upon "educational or other purposes". A Committee has been inquiring in China as to the best way of spending the money. All the British whom the Committee saw in China opposed the spending of the money upon educational purposes, presumably on the ground that nothing but ignorance can prevent the Chinese from being anti-British. I have seen no announcement in the British Press as to how the money is to be spent, but the following is probably substantially correct (*Far Eastern Times*, May 28,1926):-

> According to the *Chen Pao*, the British Government has decided to devote the money to the following purposes: (1) 30% for agricultural enterprises; (2) 23% for the erection of science institutes; (3) 17% for public health work; (4) the balance of 30% to be used in accordance with the recommendations of the Board of Trustees. In connection with the second item, the *Chen Pao* says that eight institutes will be established; namely — physics, botany, chemistry, geology, zoology, social sciences, history and anthropology. Regarding the position of the Board of Trustees, the *Chen Pao* says that China will have six members and Great Britain five, but that all of them will be appointed by the British Government.

The Chinese object to the continued British control, which makes British behaviour in the matter compare unfavourably with that of America. Also they would have wished the money spent wholly on educational purposes. The work on public health will of course not include birth-control, and will therefore be wholly useless, for reasons suggested on page 73 above. Nevertheless, the above scheme is not so bad as it might be; it may do some good and not much harm.

The events of the last few years have greatly increased the gravity of the outlook. It now seems highly probable that the Powers will continue to bully China until that country is forced into militarism, and that when that day comes all foreigners except Russians will be driven into the sea, while the Chinese themselves, by acquiring all our vices, will lose the qualities which have earned them the respect and affection of all who knew them well. For this disaster, the greatest share of the responsibility, except during the years of the war, will fall to the lot of the British. Would that it were not so!

August, 1926

# INDEX

Note: Page numbers followed by "n" denote endnotes.

Printed in the United States
by Baker & Taylor Publisher Services